**CINÉ-FILES: The French Film Guides**
Series Editor: Ginette Vincendeau

From the pioneering days of the Lumière brothers' Cinématographe in 1895, France has been home to perhaps the most consistently vibrant film culture in the world, producing world-class directors and stars, and a stream of remarkable movies, from popular genre films to cult avant-garde works. Many of these have found a devoted audience outside France, and the arrival of DVD is now enabling a whole new generation to have access to contemporary titles as well as the great classics of the past.

The Ciné-Files French Film Guides build on this welcome new access, offering authoritative and entertaining guides to some of the most significant titles, from the silent era to the early 21st century. Written by experts in French cinema, the books combine extensive research with the author's distinctive, sometimes provocative perspective on each film. The series will thus build up an essential collection on great French classics, enabling students, teachers and lovers of French cinema both to learn more about their favourite films and make new discoveries in one of the world's richest bodies of cinematic work.

Ginette Vincendeau

The first Ciné-Files, publishing 2005, are:
*Alphaville* (Jean-Luc Godard, 1965) – Chris Darke
*Les Diaboliques* (Henri-Georges Clouzot, 1955) – Susan Hayward
*La Haine* (Mathieu Kassovitz, 1995) – Ginette Vincendeau
*La Reine Margot* (Patrice Chéreau, 1994) – Julianne Pidduck

Forthcoming Ciné-Files include:
*Amélie* (Jean-Pierre Jeunet, 2001) – Isabelle Vanderschelden
*La Règle du jeu* (Jean Renoir, 1939) – Keith Reader
*Le Corbeau* (Henri-Georges Clouzot, 1943) – Judith Mayne
*Casque d'or* (Jacques Becker, 1952) – Sarah Leahy
*Cléo de 5 à 7* (Agnès Varda, 1961) – Valerie Orpen
*Rififi* (Jules Dassin, 1955) – Alastair Phillips
*La Grande illusion* (Jean Renoir, 1937) – Martin O'Shaughnessy
*Un chien andalou* (Luis Buñuel, 1929) – Elza Adamowicz
*À bout de souffle* (Jean-Luc Godard, 1960) – Ramona Fotiade

# La Reine Margot

## (Patrice Chéreau, 1994)

### Julianne Pidduck

I.B. TAURIS

LONDON · NEW YORK

Published in 2005 by I.B.Tauris & Co. Ltd

6 Salem Road, London W2 4BU

175 Fifth Avenue, New York NY 10010

ibtauris.com

ISBN: 1 84511 215 6 (hb)

EAN: 978 1 84511 215 8 (hb)

ISBN: 1 84511 100 1 (pb)

EAN: 978 1 84511 100 7 (pb)

A full CIP record for this book is available from the British Library

Typeset in Minion by Dexter Haven Associates Ltd, London

Printed and bound in Great Britain by TJ International Ltd, Padstow, Cornwall

# Contents

# Acknowledgements

I gratefully acknowledge the organisers of the Popular European Cinema 2 conference (March 2000) for providing me with the opportunity to present this research at an early stage; I am greatly indebted to the generous comments from conference participants that helped to shape this project. Also, the productive feedback for an autumn 2000 seminar paper from my colleagues in the broader Institute for Cultural Research (ICR) at Lancaster University has been (as always) most stimulating.

The research for this project was greatly enabled by a Faculty of Social Sciences Research Support Grant from Lancaster University. Also much appreciated is the contribution of the team at I.B. Tauris, especially Philippa Brewster, Gretchen Ladish and Clare Dubois.

A huge debt of thanks is also due to Ginette Vincendeau for her encouragement, tremendous intellectual generosity and warm hospitality and humour: Ginette's contribution to this project has been immeasurable. Further, I wish to mention that Geneviève Sellier's incisive observations on both versions of *La Reine Margot* have been pivotal to this work, as has the historical research of Éliane Viennot.

Cheers to Janine Grenfell, whose support in the ICR has been indispensable. I would also like to thank Bev and Doug Pidduck for their lively interest and the expertise that they have brought to this book. Finally, many thanks to Anick Druelle for her aid in the finer points of French translation, her genuine appreciation of costume film and her wonderful support throughout.

# Synopsis

As a preface, an intertitle announces the date as August 1572, the eve of a wedding between the Catholic princess Marguerite de Valois ('Margot', the sister of King Charles IX) and Protestant leader Henri de Navarre. We are informed that this wedding has been arranged to secure peace between the French Protestants (known as 'Huguenots') and Catholics in the midst of the Wars of Religion. Thousands of Protestants have come to Paris for the event, and the titles announce ominously that 'Margot's wedding, a symbol of peace and reconciliation, will be used to set off the greatest massacre in the history of France'. The action of *La Reine Margot* begins with the meeting of the Protestant La Môle and Catholic Coconnas, who, due to the overcrowding of Paris for the royal wedding, are forced to share a bed at an inn. Immediately afterwards, the spectacular wedding sequence between Margot and Navarre takes place. Despite the reconciliation of France promised by this wedding, the ceremony and subsequent festivities are marred by deep tensions.

The wedding festivities are steeped in violence and sexual desire. Margot and her friend Henriette openly scan the party for handsome Protestant lovers, while on the orders of Catherine de Médicis (the queen mother) the lovely young Charlotte de Sauve propositions Navarre. Meanwhile, the powerful Huguenot leader Admiral Coligny proposes that Navarre join his campaign in the Netherlands against Catholic Spain; later the admiral convinces the king to endorse the war effort. Subsequently, Médicis commissions the assassin Maurevel to assassinate Coligny, whose influence with the king challenges her own position. Finally, Navarre is baited by the powerful and hostile Catholics Anjou (the king's brother and next in line to the throne) and Henri de Guise (one of Margot's lovers). Indeed, Margot has already invited Guise to her chambers on her wedding night, 'as usual'.

During the wedding night Margot and Guise begin to make love in the princess's chambers, only to be interrupted by Navarre, who asks Margot to act as his ally. From this conversation, and a previous exchange during the wedding party, it is agreed that Margot will not sleep with her husband, and Navarre departs. Afterwards, the jealous Guise (who has been hiding in an antechamber) leaves Margot alone on her wedding night, and the bride declares to Henriette: 'I need a man tonight.' The two masked women trawl the streets of Paris seeking a suitable mate for Margot, meeting La Môle as his horse and possessions are stolen. Margot propositions him to have sex with her in an alleyway. Afterwards, La Môle pawns a valuable falconry book inscribed with the name of his father 'Leyrac de la Môle'. He learns from the bookseller René (who also happens to be the queen's perfume-maker and poisoner) that Coligny has been shot. Political tensions erupt in the streets in the wake of the attempted assassination.

In the build-up to the massacre, different factions respond to the crisis. Margot, sensing danger for the Protestant visitors, warns Navarre and his lieutenants to flee Paris immediately, but they ignore her advice. Médicis, Anjou and Guise seek to convince the king that he must strike first against the Huguenots in order to avoid reprisals for Coligny. At first, Anjou names 10 to 15 Protestant leaders to be eliminated. The weak king breaks under the pressure, declaring that Coligny must die, alongside 'all of the others in France'. Drafting soldiers to carry out the killing, the arch-Catholic Guise interprets the king's ambiguous orders to the extreme, and a limited attack on the Huguenot leaders spreads out into the streets of Paris.

The violence begins as the king's soldiers burst in on the Huguenot leaders, many of whom are immediately executed while Navarre is led away. In the Louvre the killing escalates, as Nançay (captain of the guard) leads a vicious attack on Huguenot women and men. Meanwhile, in the streets of Paris, Coconnas (now one of the Catholic henchmen) returns to the inn to attack La Môle. Each man is injured in the exchange, and La Môle escapes. As the carnage continues, the badly injured La Môle makes his way to Margot's chambers. Recognising him as her lover from the streets, Margot nurses his wounds and protects him against the soldiers. As Margot is called to Navarre's side, La Môle leaves the Louvre in pursuit of Coconnas, and a protracted swordfight ensues. Later, as corpses are transported to the outskirts of Paris for mass burial, the two gravely injured men are rescued by the executioner, who will nurse them back to health.

The next section of the film traces the political and personal intrigue in the aftermath of the massacre. Navarre is forced to convert to Catholicism, and is kept under house arrest at the Louvre along with Margot, who has angered her family by siding with the Protestants. At this time Médicis is shown consulting her poisoner René, who reads the Valois' destiny in the entrails of an animal. He predicts the early death of Médicis' three remaining sons and Navarre's eventual succession to the throne. This prediction galvanises several attacks on Navarre by Médicis, the first of which involves poisoning the lip rouge of Sauve, Navarre's lover. As a result, the young woman dies horribly, but Navarre survives thanks to Margot's intervention.

Meanwhile, the recovered La Môle sets out to Amsterdam to meet up with French survivors of the massacre (notably Armagnac and Condé), seeking to secure Dutch support for a Huguenot uprising. With the help of Mendès (a Spanish Jew exiled in Amsterdam), a plot is hatched to free Navarre, who is to slip away during a wild boar hunt. Upon his return to Paris, La Môle finds Coconnas recovered and living with Margot's friend Henriette; riddled with guilt for his role in the massacre, Coconnas embraces La Môle as a friend and helps him to reunite with Margot. After a tender lover's tryst, they agree that Margot will flee the Louvre while Navarre makes his escape.

The hunt marks the film's third major spectacular set piece, featuring men on horseback galloping through the forest. As the dogs corner the wild boar, the king is thrown from his mount and finds himself under attack from the boar. The opportunistic Anjou prevents the other members of the hunt from intervening, and they all watch silently as the king faces the boar's attack alone. At this very moment, La Môle and Coconnas signal Navarre to join the Huguenot forces assembled nearby, but he chooses to rescue the king instead. This act marks a turning point in Navarre's fortunes, as he misses his chance to escape but gains the king's protection.

Back at the Louvre, the king protects Navarre – his new favourite – from Médicis' assassin Maurevel. Not so lucky is Navarre's supporter Armagnac, who is quietly dispatched by Maurevel. Meanwhile, Margot and Henriette have escaped the Louvre to await La Môle in a country manor away from Paris. When La Môle arrives he informs her that the plot has failed, and that she must return to the capital. They make love for the last time that night, and Margot and Henriette return to Paris.

Meanwhile, back at the Louvre, Charles shows a different side of himself by inviting Navarre to sup with his mistress and child. Livid at Navarre's newfound favour, Médicis poisons the falconry book that La Môle had previously sold to René. With the knowledge of her youngest son Alençon, the poisoned book is left for Navarre, but it is the king who finds it. Some time later, at the farewell party for Anjou (who is being sent to Poland after his betrayal of the king at the hunt), Navarre is taunted by Anjou, and, when Margot intervenes, Guise, Anjou and Alençon manhandle her. The Valois brothers show the court the 'marks' that each of them had made on her body when they molested her as children. This disturbing scene is cut short by Charles' sudden collapse. Regaining his composure, the king finds his beloved dog Actéon dead from chewing on the poisoned book. During the autopsy of the dog, Charles learns that his mother had poisoned the book with Navarre as the intended victim – and that he will die an agonising death.

After this realisation, the king allows Navarre to escape the Louvre during a hunting expedition, but refuses to allow Margot to accompany her husband to Navarre. The next scene shows the king on his deathbed, writhing in pain and sweating blood. From Charles' bedside, the action shifts to Navarre back in his own kingdom, as he renews his Protestant faith. Also in Navarre are La Môle and Coconnas, who volunteer to return to Paris to fetch Margot. However, upon their arrival in Paris, they are ambushed and arrested by Guise and his men. In the film's final scenes Margot pleads with the dying king to pardon La Môle. Accusing his sister of neglecting him in his illness, Charles refuses to pardon La Môle (who has been accused of murdering the king because the poisoned book bore his father's name).

Early on the morning of Charles' death, Coconnas and La Môle are both decapitated by the executioner who had cared for them after the massacre. At this time Anjou returns to Paris to be named Henri III of France, while Margot and Henriette mourn their dead lovers. Margot asks the undertaker to embalm La Môle's head, and the film closes on Margot leaving Paris in a carriage with the page Orthon.

Full credits for *La Reine Margot* can be found in Appendix 1.

# Introduction

Patrice Chéreau's 1994 film *La Reine Margot* paints a vivid canvas of Renaissance political intolerance and intrigue. Based on Alexandre Dumas' Romantic novel of 1844, the film was conceived as a cinematic 'event' featuring the elusive star Isabelle Adjani in the leading role of the 16th-century princess Marguerite de Valois (immortalised in popular memory by Dumas' novel as '*la reine Margot*'). As a greatly anticipated popular film and a critically acclaimed auteurist work, *La Reine Margot* is a key French film of the 1990s. Its economy of scale and spectacular cinematography coincide with a cycle of late 1980s and early 1990s French historical 'super-productions', including *Cyrano de Bergerac, Germinal* and *Le Hussard sur le toit*. Partially supported by state funds from the government of President François Mitterrand, these works mobilise 'mythic' elements of French history and culture for contemporary audiences.

*La Reine Margot* works from two major mythologies. Firstly, Dumas' novel and, in turn, Chéreau's adaptation represent the 1572 massacre of Saint-Barthélemy, where thousands of French Protestants were slaughtered in the Louvre and on the streets of Paris. Famously, the massacre took place after the royal wedding between the Catholic princess Marguerite de Valois (sister of Charles IX) and the Protestant Henri de Navarre (later Henri IV of France). Ironically, the wedding had been brokered to secure peace between religious factions amidst the Wars of Religion, and many of the victims were wedding guests. The second mythology concerns Adjani's eagerly awaited performance as the iconic 'Margot' – a Renaissance princess best remembered (perhaps unjustly so) for her alleged voracious sexual appetites. Placing this sexual female protagonist with an infamous episode of sectarian violence, Chéreau's film is renowned for its violent and erotic depiction of the French national past.

This film guide examines the film's production and reception, and provides a detailed reading of the film. Chapter 1 explores the contexts of the film's production – the 16th-century historical context, the legacy of Romanticism and Dumas' novel, and the industrial backdrop and creative players involved in the film's production. Chapter 2 presents an extended reading of the film, with an emphasis on the film's cinematic spectacle of violence and its corporeal codes of gender and sexuality. Finally, Chapter 3 analyses the reception of *La Reine Margot* in France and internationally, where Chéreau's auteurist work has received widespread critical acclaim.

# 1 Production contexts

Patrice Chéreau's *La Reine Margot* belongs to a cycle of epic French costume films from the late 1980s, including *Camille Claudel* (1988), *Cyrano de Bergerac* (1989), *Germinal* (1992), *Indochine* (1992), *L'Amant* (1992), *Le Colonel Chabert* (1994) and *Le Hussard sur le toit/The Horseman on the Roof* (1995). As part of the French film industry's return to literary adaptations and historical films, these prestigious 'super-productions' are conceived as a kind of cinematic event. They present lavish period spectacles offering a wide array of cinematic pleasures: scenic landscapes and period cityscapes, adaptations of classic French literature and theatre, reconstructions of historical milieux and events fleshed out with hundreds or even thousands of extras, lush cinematography and sweeping musical scores, star-studded French and international casts, beautiful period costumes, décor and furnishings.

As with *Cyrano de Bergerac* and *Germinal*, the cultural 'value' of *La Reine Margot* arises from its epic cinematic qualities, and also from an array of iconic references drawn from French classical and popular culture. Most important of these is the Romantic novel *La Reine Margot* by Alexandre Dumas (père),[1] which helped to crystallise a popular mythology of the beautiful 'queen Margot' based on the Renaissance princess Marguerite de Valois. Dumas' novel and the 1994 adaptation foreground this figure, and the participation of the glamorous, bankable star Isabelle Adjani in the lead role of Margot was crucial to the film's financing and its high-profile release. As I will argue below, the 'mythic' doubling of the historical figure of Valois and Adjani's contemporary star persona generates much of the allure of Chéreau's production. Long before the film's release, the film was heralded in the French press as a prestigious Dumas adaptation with Adjani in the iconic role of Margot under the direction of the respected avant-garde theatre director Chéreau.

This chapter examines several key contexts of production for *La Reine Margot*. These include the film's historical referents of the Wars of Religion and the massacre of Saint-Barthélemy (St Bartholomew's Day Massacre) of 1572, the socio-political context of 1990s France, Dumas and the French Romantics as literary and stylistic sources, the mythology surrounding Marguerite de Valois, Adjani's star persona, Chéreau's background as theatre and film director, French traditions of historical film production, the French film industry of the 1990s – and, finally, the film's cast and crew. All these frames of reference contribute to the film's complex industrial, cultural, political and aesthetic resonances.

### Historical contexts: Renaissance France and contemporary France

*La Reine Margot* represents significant historical events of Renaissance France, notably the infamous 1572 massacre of Saint-Barthélemy. A bloody episode of sectarian violence, the massacre epitomises the terrible consequences of religious intolerance in France during the Counter-Reformation.[2] Between 1562 and 1585 the minority French Protestants (known as Huguenots) were engaged in a protracted struggle with the dominant Catholic forces in eight separate Wars of Religion. (For the dates of these and other historical events of the period, see the historical timeline in Appendix 2.) The troubled period of the Wars of Religion coincided with the final decades of the Valois dynasty, when the Italian matriarch Catherine de Médicis and her two sons (Charles IX and Henri III) presided over a divided, unstable and violent France.

*La Reine Margot* begins with the marriage between Marguerite de Valois (the younger sister of the Valois king Charles IX) and the Protestant Henri, king of Navarre. The union between the Catholic princess and the Huguenot leader had been brokered to secure the 1570 Peace of Saint-

Germain, a truce signed between Catholic and Protestant factions to resolve the third War of Religion. Many of the most important Huguenot leaders and their followers streamed into Paris from all over the realm to attend the wedding. The wedding took place on 18 August 1572, and a few days later amidst the festivities the majority Catholics turned on the Protestant 'heretics'. During the night of 24 August the violence began in the Louvre (the royal palace that is the setting for much of the film's action); the injured Coligny was murdered by Guise himself, while several dozen Huguenot leaders were assassinated by the king's Swiss guards and Anjou's personal bodyguards.[3] Subsequently the violence spread to the streets of Paris. While most of the killing took place in Paris between August 24 and 28, the violence spread sporadically to the outlying provinces in the following weeks. Depending on the affiliations of the record-keepers, the number of Protestant casualties has been estimated anywhere from 2,000 to 10,000, or even more.[4]

The centrepiece of Chéreau's film, the massacre of Saint-Barthélemy, is held in popular memory as the bloodiest sectarian event of the French Counter-Reformation amidst a protracted period of political and religious strife. Historian N.M. Sutherland attributes the massacre to the convergence of several factors.[5] One significant factor was the gradual collapse and subsequent weakness of the Valois monarchy after the sudden deaths of Henri II in 1559 and his heir François II in 1560. After François' sudden death, the child king Charles IX came to power under the regency of his mother Catherine de Médicis. The power vacuum in the wake of Henri II's strong rule was exacerbated by infighting between Charles (a weak and indecisive king even after his age of majority) and his two younger brothers, Henri, duc d'Anjou and François, duc d'Alençon. Charles reigned until his death from tuberculosis in 1574 – not from poison, as alleged in Dumas' novel and its adaptation. At this nexus that corresponds to the film's dénouement, Anjou was crowned Henri III of France. The last of the Valois dynasty, Catherine de Médicis and her three younger sons, along with her daughter Marguerite (and Marguerite's husband Henri de Navarre, who will later become king of France), make up the core *dramatis personae* of Chéreau's film.

During the unstable period of the French Counter-Reformation the weakness of the monarchy did nothing to discourage bitter rivalries among the powerful nobility, who sought to control the French crown and the influential advisory council.[6] Aristocratic families or whole provinces championed either the Catholic or Protestant cause, often challenging the authority of the monarchy. The Wars of Religion arose in the wake of considerable inroads for Calvinism within France. Although the Protestant heretics were persecuted, the power balance shifted as important members of the high nobility were converted, including Coligny, the Condé family, Antoine de Bourbon and his son Henri de Navarre.

Contesting the rising power of the Protestant nobility, Catholic dynasties such as the Guise family (represented in the film by Henri, duc de Guise, one of Margot's lovers) supported an intolerant Catholic policy that would impose death on all Protestant 'heretics'. The Guise family was engaged in bitter rivalries with powerful Protestants, including Gaspard de Châtillon, sire de Coligny, the king's adviser (known in the film as Admiral Coligny). Political assassinations were rampant in this period, and Coligny had been implicated in the 1563 murder of François, father of Henri, duc de Guise. In fact, as portrayed in the film, it is the botched assassination of Coligny on 22 August 1572 (a few days after the royal wedding) that sparked off the massacre two days later.

Within this fraught historical conjuncture, the international political context of these events is perhaps the most difficult aspect of the film to grasp. During the latter part of the 16th century Europe was dominated by three powerful figures: Elizabeth I of England, Philip II of Spain[7] – and in France the Italian Catherine de Médicis, widow of Henri II and mother of three young kings. Controlled by these giant historical figures, the three nations were embroiled in a struggle for political control in an embattled Europe where politics were inextricable from religion. In England Elizabeth I took power in 1558, and followed her father Henry VIII's policies to reinstitute Anglicanism as the state religion. The close interconnection of these nations and their rulers is exemplified by the story of Mary Stuart, Queen of Scots, who was married to French King François II. Upon his sudden death in 1560 Mary returned to Scotland representing a rival Scottish (and Catholic) claim to the English throne. Elizabeth I imprisoned and eventually executed her rival.

Meanwhile, Philip II of Spain and the Catholic Church, based in Rome, mounted a virulent defence of Catholicism in contest with the spread of Protestantism across Europe. Philip II and Popes Pius IV and Pius V intervened actively within French domestic affairs to fuel the Wars of Religion. For instance, they supported the arch-Catholic faction called the Triumvirate (later the Holy League), spearheaded by the Guise family; Anjou, the younger brother of Charles IX, was associated with this group. During this period the power of the Spaniards was seen to threaten the security of both France and England; in fact, Spain held an important foothold in northern Europe in the United Provinces – the present-day Netherlands.

From the 1560s onwards, there was strong Dutch Calvinist resistance to repressive Spanish occupation. Given the close links between the Dutch and French Protestants, Philip II feared that the powerful French Huguenots would support a revolt in the Netherlands. Indeed, as depicted in the film, Protestant leaders such as Coligny, Condé, de Nassau and Téligny tried to persuade Charles IX to join an anti-Spanish 'Netherlands Enterprise' in concert with England and the Dutch Protestant leader William of Orange.[8] Significantly, Coligny, Nassau and Téligny were all executed in the massacre, and for Sutherland one major outcome of Saint-Barthélemy was the defeat of the Netherlands Enterprise. The alliance between French and Dutch Protestants is depicted in the film through the journey of La Môle (Margot's Huguenot lover) to Amsterdam after the massacre.[9]

This international context of political and religious strife helped to further destabilise an already divided France that had been reduced to a state of national bankruptcy after a decade of civil war. At this time the modern doctrine of religious tolerance was virtually unknown, and the Huguenots were widely hated and feared. After the Peace of Saint-Germain in 1570, the Huguenots formed a strong military and political community wielding considerable influence. Part of the threat that they posed was due to their religious doctrine, which had taken increasingly anti-monarchist tones since the 1560s. In addition to 'heretical' religious practices, this challenge to the sacral monarchy was highly threatening to many French Catholics.[10] As a result of these factors, the Huguenots became a vilified minority commonly scapegoated for the nation's ills, which included an increased burden of taxation – specifically a 40% increase in the price of cereal food staples during the summer of 1572.[11]

Returning to the events with which the film begins, Paris in the summer of 1572 was a city rife with political, religious and economic unrest. The wedding between Navarre and Marguerite de Valois took place in an already crowded Paris packed with Huguenot visitors at the hottest time of the year. Brewing tensions erupted with the attack on the Protestant leader Coligny (who was also hated for his influence on the king). After the attempted assassination the Huguenots clamoured for justice against Coligny's attackers, while in the streets of Paris a deep hatred of the heretics was rampant among the Catholic majority. As noted above, on 24 August most of the Huguenot leaders were assassinated. Only a few were spared, including the bridegroom Navarre (who was also in line for the French throne through his mother, Jeanne d'Albrêt); in order to avoid the fate of his supporters, Navarre was forced to convert to Catholicism.

The question of the responsibility for the attacks on Coligny and the Huguenot leaders remains a contested point among historians. Chéreau's film follows Dumas' novel in blaming the Valois monarchy, notably the influential Italian Catherine de Médicis, who was seen to control her weak son Charles IX. However, Sutherland insists that Médicis consistently sought to maintain peace through policies of religious tolerance.[12] For this historian, the massacre was not a premeditated act, but resulted from several factors that developed over a long period. On this account, the Valois monarchy (in consultation with the royal council) dispatched the Huguenot leaders in a desperate measure to prevent civil war. The spread of the violence outside the Louvre was the unhappy result of widespread social unrest, and also perhaps (as the film suggests) resulting from the common belief that the king had sanctioned the violence. Mark P. Holt notes that the massacre was characterised by horrific acts (including the 'unusually harsh treatment of women').

> Viewed by Catholics as threats to the social and political order, Huguenots not only had to be exterminated...they also had to be humiliated, dishonoured, and shamed as the inhuman beasts that they were perceived to be. The victims had to be dehumanized – slaughtered like animals – since they had violated all the sacred laws of humanity in Catholic culture.[13]

With an intensive focus on the massacre, *La Reine Margot* follows the narrative framework of Dumas' novel to depict the massacre and its aftermath until the death of Charles IX, two years later. In the next section, I provide a brief account of the complex aftermath of Saint-Barthélemy. Given the tremendous complexity of this period, my schematic account will foreground the roles of the film's major protagonists. La Môle, the film's romantic lead, was an actual historical figure reputed to be the princess's lover. Joseph de

Boniface, seigneur de La Môle, was a servant and a favourite of Alençon (youngest brother of Marguerite and Charles IX). La Môle was involved in a Protestant alliance called the Malcontents (later the Politiques). Contesting the fanatical Catholic Holy League, the Politiques developed a nationalist policy of religious tolerance in response to interventions by Spain and Rome. Associated with Navarre and Marguerite de Valois, the party promoted Alençon as the next king in the place of Anjou (who was aligned with the arch-Catholic faction).

In 1574, as Charles IX lay on his deathbed, a plot by the Politiques was discovered. The royal conspirators escaped conviction, but La Môle and his friend Annibal de Coconnas were captured, tortured and finally decapitated.[14] (Within historical records, these two men were rumoured to be lovers of Marguerite and her friend Henriette de Clèves, duchesse de Nevers; the minor historical figures of La Môle, Coconnas and Henriette have been immortalised by Dumas' novel.) Marguerite de Valois was also associated with the Politiques, acting as intermediary between Navarre and Alençon.[15] In 1577 she travelled to Flanders as ambassador of the alliance to convince the Dutch rebels in conflict with Philip of Spain to choose Alençon as their sovereign.

The moderate political alternative proposed by the Politiques waned with Alençon's death in 1584. In the final years of the 16th century the Valois dynasty fell into decline, as all four of Catherine de Médicis' sons died young and without legitimate heirs. After the assassination of Henri III (Charles IX's successor) in 1589, Navarre was next in line for the French throne. The first of the Bourbon kings, Henri IV reigned for 12 years until his assassination in 1610. Remembered fondly in French history as 'Good King Henri', the converted Huguenot was the architect of the famous Edict of Nantes of 1598 that granted Protestants 'freedom of conscience, equality of rights and the freedom to worship in numerous specified places'.[16]

Meanwhile, the fortunes of Marguerite de Valois foundered with Alençon's death and her subsequent estrangement from Catherine de Médicis, Henri III and her husband. She was sequestered from political life in a fortress at Usson from 1586 until 1605, where she pursued her extensive interest in literature and the arts and began to write her *Mémoires*. Her marriage with Henri IV was annulled in 1599, and Marguerite was granted the title of 'la reine Marguerite'. After the divorce Henri IV married Marie de Médicis, a distant cousin of Catherine de Médicis who gave birth to his heir Louis XIII in 1600. Returning to Paris (and public life) in 1605, Marguerite de Valois enjoyed popularity for fostering political stability in France after the murder of Henri IV until her death in 1615. The 'reine Marguerite' offered her unwavering support for the child king Louis XIII and the regent Marie de Médicis.[17] (I will return below to the mythology of Marguerite de Valois.)

Dumas' novel and Chéreau's adaptation address the tumultuous period of the mid-16th century. The majority of the French audience would be aware of the subsequent tolerant policies of Henri IV, but this violent period – and particularly the massacre of Saint-Barthélemy – dominates the film's visceral and spectacular historical vision. Denis Crouzet argues that the massacre marks a watershed in French history, 'exceeding the limited period of the Wars of Religion and the brief moments of August 1572; and it is for this reason that the inhuman and barbaric night of 24 August 1572 will be recalled as the event among the events of a long 16th century – that it will condense all the fears and passions, resentments and aspirations that for a long time will mark the key stakes within the French memory'.[18]

*La Reine Margot* returns to this period of religious intolerance from the vantage point of a secular modern France. Henri IV's subsequent Edict of Nantes eased the religious strife of the French Counter-Reformation.[19] However, a century later Louis XIV's 1685 Revocation of the Edict of Nantes reversed this tolerant policy, once again imposing repressive sanctions against the Huguenot minority; of nearly 1,000,000 French Protestants, at least 100,000 chose exile.[20] Eventually, the *Ancien Régime*'s structuring conflict between Catholicism and Protestantism was largely eclipsed by the French Revolution. Since the 19th century a republican commitment to a secular state has offset the powers of the Catholic Church,[21] but within contemporary secular France the memory of repression lingers on among French Protestants.[22]

In the 20th century, the spectre of religious intolerance within France resurfaced with anti-semitism and the renewed rise of the National Front from the 1980s. A touchstone event within French history, public debate surrounding anti-semitism first arose in France when Captain Alfred Dreyfus, a Jewish officer in the French army, was unjustly accused of spying for Germany in 1894. At this time the Catholic Church and other conservative forces took a position against the Jewish officer, whereas the republicans were associated with Dreyfus's defence; this political landscape underscored the necessity for a separation of Church and state within France.[23] The question of anti-semitism arose again with the post-war interrogation of the Vichy régime's responsibility for the treatment of the French Jews during the Second World War. At the time of the film's release there was a belated public acknowledgement of the Vichy government's role in the Holocaust. In 1993, for instance, the first Sunday after 16 July[24] was designated a national day for the memory of victims of racist and anti-semitic persecutions committed under the authority of the Vichy government.

Chéreau's return to the massacre of Saint-Barthélemy evokes the horrors of intolerance and genocide across different historical periods. *La Reine Margot* appeared at a time when xenophobia, racism and religious intolerance were on the rise in France, notably with the increased visibility of the National Front. Even as the French political climate of the 16th century was profoundly shaped by international factors, the rise of the extreme Right in France is linked with broader European contexts of intolerance and sectarian violence. In fact, Chéreau's treatment of the 1572 massacre was explicitly framed as a response to the religious violence in the Balkans in the 1980s and 1990s; the film was released shortly after the atrocities in Rwanda, which were also mentioned in interviews and reviews.

Like many of the French historical 'super-productions' of the late 1980s and early 1990s (*Le Colonel Chabert, Le Hussard sur le toit, Germinal*), *La Reine Margot* returns to a troubled period in the national past. Chéreau's film was produced in the twilight of the Mitterrand government (1981–1995) at a time of widespread disappointment with the Socialist experiment. For Ginette Vincendeau, the films' persistent return to historical periods of violence and instability suggests a deep unease within the society that produced the film.

> The contemporary recourse in films to Balzac's [*Germinal*] and Dumas' mediations of the past must also be seen in the light of struggles over French national identity, which a conflation of factors are destabilising: the passing of the last great populist leader (Charles de Gaulle), the end of the *trente glorieuses* years of economic boom, the demise of the colonial empire and the rise of multiculturalism.[25]

Perhaps an indication of an uncertain national present haunted by intolerance and instability, there is a chord of deep pessimism running through *La Reine Margot*. Chéreau's distinctive auteurist rendering of a bloody 16th century builds upon the dark, turbulent Romantic aesthetic suggested by Dumas' source novel and other stylistic influences.

## Representing the past: Romanticism and other references

Fictionalised accounts of actual historical events and figures raise a series of historiographical questions. In the transition from the complexity of historical forces and events to fictional representation, how is the past interpreted? How are collective memories shaped by fictional representations of the past conveyed in literature, paintings, film and television? How do these cultural dramatisations of past events address contemporary social and cultural discourses? These questions are explored within an extensive scholarship that delineates the transition from historical events to narrative dramatisations of the past.

*La Reine Margot* can be categorised as a hybrid of costume film (or what is called '*le film en costume*' in France) and 'historical fiction'. The costume film foregrounds fantastical private experiences (notably romance) within non-realist past settings, whereas the 'historical film' seeks to represent more directly actual historical events. The historical film, with its treatment of 'official' history, is often attributed greater cultural value by film critics than the more 'feminine' or 'escapist' form of costume drama. For instance, Robert A. Rosenstone distinguishes between 'historical fiction' that engages, 'directly or obliquely, with the issues, ideas, data, and arguments of the ongoing discourse of history' and costume drama that 'uses the past as an exotic setting for romance and adventure'.[26] As I will elaborate below, this gendered dismissal of costume film arises dramatically in French critical debates around the 1950s' 'tradition of quality'.

One persistent critique insists that the fictional and dramatic elements of 'costume film' obscure historical accuracy. In contrast, a 'revisionist' view suggests that representations of the past produce meanings in the present of the film's production and reception. As François de la Bretèque suggests,

> If these films teach us nothing about the historical societies they are supposed to represent and a great deal on the other hand about the contemporary contexts of their production, the most interesting insights can be found in the

contrast between these two time-frames. Meanings are produced through contrast, rather than through a simple logic of transposition.[27]

The predominant approach to historical representation used in this book follows this revisionist position to address how *La Reine Margot* constructs meanings in the present through mythology and intertextuality. In keeping with my own work and the approaches of Raphael Samuel, François de la Bretèque and Marcia Landy,[28] this perspective explores how popular culture forms (including film) use past settings and stories to engage symbolically with cultural and political issues in the present.

Framed in this way, the events of August 1572 are embedded within the French national memory as a moment of sectarian violence within the turbulent 16th century. Here, another conceptual project of particular relevance is Pierre Nora's *Les Lieux de mémoire*. This work addresses the 'places' or 'sites', 'whether material or non-material in nature, which by dint of human will or the work of time [have] become a symbolic element of the national heritage'.[29] I would suggest that the massacre of Saint-Barthélemy marks an important 'place of memory' within contemporary France – an event metonymically marking the terrible repercussions of religious intolerance. As a popular cultural text, Chéreau's film and other historical 'super-productions' intervene as 'memory-images' within the field of cultural memory, rather than as repositories of historical 'truth'. The gap between history and memory is part of a broader cultural condition sometimes associated with postmodernity. For Nora, the accelerated, future-oriented temporality of modernity has displaced deep-rooted traditions of social memory with 'a memory of a past that eternally recycles a heritage, relegating ancestral yesterdays to the undifferentiated time of heroes, inceptions, and myth'.[30]

One of the implications of this revisionist historiography is that cultural audiences and cultural producers never have direct or unmediated access to historical events; 'places of memory' have been continually encoded through cultural practices and representations. In order to depict the massacre, Chéreau's film draws from an immense body of cultural references and myths. Danièle Thompson's script and Chéreau's direction rely heavily upon the Romantic themes running through Dumas' novel, which narrates the historical events of the Renaissance through 19th-century discourses and aesthetics. Notably, Chéreau draws from French Romantic literature

(Dumas) and painting (Delacroix) – and from the Elizabethan drama (Marlowe, Shakespeare) that strongly influenced the French Romantics' vision of the Renaissance.

Given that recent French historical films (*Cyrano de Bergerac, Le Bossu* and the many adaptations of Dumas including *La Reine Margot*) often represent the *Ancien Régime* through the cultural imaginary of Romanticism, it is useful to examine this formative movement more closely. The Romantic period corresponds with a period of intense social and political upheaval across Europe, notably the French Revolution and the Industrial Revolution. In this respect, Romanticism marks a significant cultural and intellectual response to the rise of modernity, where everyday life is marked by industrialisation and the 'shock of the new'. Romantic artists frequently returned to medieval and Renaissance periods (and also to exotic or 'Oriental' locations) to seek inspiration far from the complexities of the political present. Here, we can find a parallel with contemporary period filmmaking, which is often accused of fleeing from the difficult present into nostalgic fantasies of the past.

French Romanticism belongs to a broader European wave of art and thought emerging between 1789 and 1848. In general terms, the movement marks a break from Enlightenment rationalist thought and the formal perfection of neoclassicist aesthetics. Instead, the Romantics elevate chaos over order, celebrating the power of individual creative expression and imagination.[31] Far from being an isolated historical sensibility, the Romantic vision persists in contemporary culture. This sensibility is a guiding force in Chéreau's cinematic vision of the past framed through the prism of visceral sensory experience.

Chéreau's film is strongly influenced by the cultural fantasy of the *Ancien Régime* developed by French Romantics Madame de Staël, Châteaubriand, Stendhal, Hugo, Dumas and Delacroix.[32] Notably, the French historical novel as developed by Victor Hugo, Alfred de Vigny and, later, Dumas was inspired by Sir Walter Scott's writings such as *Waverley* (1814). In this respect, Dumas' return to French historical figures and events in his novels *La Reine Margot, The Three Musketeers* and *The Man in the Iron Mask* corresponds with a wider European Romantic cultural fascination with the *Ancien Régime* of the medieval and Renaissance periods. For Stephen Bann, this fascination was especially strong among French Romantics after the Revolution, which had 'caused a break in political continuity which was liable to be transformed, on the subjective level, into a sense of estrangement and loss'.[33] Borrowing from Shakespeare and Schiller, Spanish drama and the Gothic novel, the French Romantics reimagined the *Ancien Régime* as a strange and distant past.[34]

Chéreau's film draws extensively on this 19th-century vision of the 16th century, constructing the past through the distinctive vision of Romantic literature. If *La Reine Margot* represents historical events obliquely, the film is also, importantly, an adaptation. Thompson's script closely follows Dumas' novel, which distills a ripping yarn from the vagaries of history. This narrative structure juxtaposes a love triangle and a monstrous, murderous family against the violent backdrop of the Wars of Religion and the massacre. In placing the mythic figure of Marguerite de Valois (remembered primarily for her many lovers) at the novel's epicentre, Dumas constructs a 'boudoir' account of the past rather than a more conventionally 'political' one. Margot's strange contractual relationship with her husband Navarre is juxtaposed with her love affair with the doomed La Môle – a minor historical figure elevated here to a leading role. Finally, Dumas draws upon popular myth to present the Valois family as a violent, squabbling family headed by an ominous mother, Catherine de Médicis. Claude Aziza evocatively characterises Dumas' Valois family as 'great predators':

> Catherine, the black queen, the widow, the she-wolf... with her voracious passion for her son the Duke of Anjou, the future Henri III, whom she wishes to be king. Weaving her web...sending her death squad into the alcoves, ready for everything and backing down at nothing – poisoning, cutting an animal's throat, massacre. Accidental infanticide, wasn't it already in her heart? For this weak Charles IX – the poor marionette that she manipulates at her own convenience – must disappear when he becomes an obstacle to her ambitions.[35]

Élaine Viennot notes that part of the 19th-century fascination with the Renaissance centred on famous historical female figures: Schiller's painting *Marie Stuart* (1801), Delaroche's painting *Execution of Lady Jane Grey* (1833), Scott's novel *Le Page de Marie Stuart* (1820), Hugo's play *Marie Tudor* (1833), Balzac's unfinished novel about Catherine de Médicis (begun in 1828) and Donizetti's operas *Anna Bolena* (1830) and *Maria Stuarda* (1834).[36] As we can see from Aziza's account, Dumas' novel intertwines the massacre of Saint-Barthélemy with the mythic figures of Catherine de Médicis and 'la reine Margot'. Associated with death and potent sexuality respectively, these two powerful female figures take a central and paradoxical role in the novel and its adaptation. Themes of gender, sexuality and death are central to *La Reine Margot*, and they will be explored at different points in this book.

In another key link with the French Romantics, Philippe Rousselot's cinematography borrows extensively from painters Delacroix and Géricault[37] – particularly their distinctive use of dark, shadowy light and dynamic tableaux of bodies caught in heroic, dynamic, violent struggles. These two painters exemplify the transition from formal, static 'classical' painting to a Romantic style emphasising 'the more sensuous qualities of paint, its colour, richness and texture'.[38] Placing greater value on the 'innately pictorial' qualities of 'colour, texture, and the enigmatic, symbolic potential of imagery',[39] Romantic painting is highly atmospheric, reflecting above all the individual expression of the artist.

Central to the cultural and commercial intertext of *La Reine Margot* are both the aura of the Romantic author (Dumas) and the Romantic ideal of (masculine) authorial genius[40] embodied in the eminent avant-garde theatre director Chéreau. Following the Romantic tradition where an author makes his own personal imprint in representing the past, *La Reine Margot* is attributed heightened cultural value through Chéreau's unique auteurist vision. For instance, *Cahiers du cinéma* critic Serge Toubiana writes: 'It is this violence, this taste of blood that makes *La Reine Margot* a film haunted by a vision – a vision that one could almost call contemporary, even as the film gives the impression of seizing historical events *live*.'[41] As I will discuss in Chapter 3, the film uneasily bridges the requirements of popular entertainment and Chéreau's auteurist aesthetics.

Best known for his work in the theatre, Chéreau has directed works by Marivaux, Koltès, Genet and Müller, as well as Shakespeare and Marlowe. In the 1970s he directed Lyon's Théâtre National Populaire, and from 1982 he has directed the Théâtre des Amandiers in Nanterre. (The Théâtre des Amandiers is listed in the credits of *La Reine Margot* as participating in the film; notably, some of the interior Louvre scenes were filmed there in specially constructed sets.) Opera is another of Chéreau's interests, and he has directed several productions, including Alban Berg's *Wozzeck* (1994) in a collaboration with Daniel Barenboim.

Prior to the release of *La Reine Margot*, Chéreau had also directed five films: *La Chair de l'orchidée*, *Judith Therpauve*, *L'Homme blessé*, *Hôtel de France* and *Le Temps et la chambre*, although it was only with *La Reine Margot* that he achieved recognition as a full-fledged cinema auteur. Additionally, Chéreau has worked as a film and theatre actor. An openly gay director, he depicts in many of his films (notably the 1983 *L'Homme blessé*, starring Jean-Hugues Anglade) intensely physical and passionate relationships among men. As I will discuss in Chapter 2, this dynamic is exemplified by *La Reine Margot*'s striking focus on the male body. Indeed, the film's vivid corporeal imagery of blood, sexuality and death was associated with the AIDS crisis, which was at its height in the early 1990s. (For Chéreau's full filmography, see Appendix 3.)[42]

As a cultural producer working across several media who has produced plays and films drawing from many different historical periods and styles, Chéreau lists many different references for *La Reine Margot*. Aside from the strong Romantic influences, specific filmic points of reference include horrific families suffused in violence and betrayal, including Coppola's *The Godfather* (1972), Scorsese's *GoodFellas* (1990) and Visconti's *The Damned* (1969) – as well as the brutality of television news.[43] An earlier filmic reference not mentioned in the film's publicity is D.W. Griffiths' dynamic spectacle of Saint-Barthélemy in the 1916 *Intolerance*. Produced in the formative early days of cinematic historical spectacle, Griffiths (along with Eisenstein) pioneered techniques of cutting between wide-angle shots of surging crowds and individual anguish captured in close-up. Chéreau's film works from these broader conventions of cinematic 'spectacle', with a particular emphasis on the expressive capacities of the close-up.

Chéreau's account of the massacre also draws from Heinrich Mann's *The Novel of Henri IV* and Marlowe's play *The Massacre at Paris* (which he directed in 1972). Drawing from his stage experience with Marlowe and Shakespeare, Chéreau's vision of the Renaissance evokes the themes and atmosphere of Elizabethan drama:

> For it is Shakespeare and Marlowe that one must find in this movie. Find the violent narration, the obvious structure, go back to the Elizabethan drama, go back to the great History, the one that crushes men and women, the one that has lost all meaning, that has become, as Shakespeare said, but 'a tale told by an idiot, full of sound and fury'.[44]

Often cited in the film's press coverage, the evocative Shakespearean passage of a 'tale of sound and fury' perfectly encapsulates the film's gripping depiction of the 1572 massacre.

### Mythologies: Catherine de Médicis and Marguerite de Valois

Within novel and film alike, the myth of Marguerite de Valois is developed through the auteurist vision of the male auteur. This legendary historical figure, as played by French star Isabelle Adjani, carries much of the glamour and the appeal of Chéreau's film. The 19th-century Romantics share with contemporary Western culture a fascination with powerful female figures, and the intermingling of past and present discourses of femininity, sexuality and power in *La Reine Margot* is of particular interest for a feminist analysis. From the Renaissance to the Romantic period to the late 20th century, we find a popular fascination with Catherine de Médicis and Marguerite de Valois, two powerful female Renaissance figures who have been mythologised within French culture.

As mentioned above, in both novel and film the powerful matriarchal figure of Médicis is rendered as unnatural mother, keeping guard over her incestuous, violent brood. Ultimately, Médicis (played brilliantly by Virna Lisi in Chéreau's film) is indicted for much of the violence within the film, including the death of her own son. Part of the long-standing lore of perversity and unbridled lust for power of the Valois dynasty, Médicis has long been vilified as a potent female historical figure and as a foreigner. The demonisation of de Médicis in France can be traced back to political pamphlets in her lifetime, notably two incendiary tracts of 1574: the *Discours merveilleux de la vie et déportements de Catherine de Médicis* and *Le Réveil-Matin des Français*. The first pamphlet attacked Médicis as a manipulative and diabolical mother who controlled her children, and convinced the king to order the massacre. The second pamphlet denounced the monstrosities of the entire royal family, evoking a depraved mother and violent, squabbling brood (including an incestuous relationship between Margot and her brother Henri).[45] The idea of the 'damned' and 'depraved' family is perpetuated in Dumas and forms the dramatic core of Chéreau's film, where it is alleged that Margot has had intercourse with each of her three brothers, with her mother's knowledge.

The images of Médicis as a predatory, controlling mother and of her daughter Marguerite as a nymphomaniac have held throughout the centuries. Within French popular memory, these two figures have long been associated with inflammatory fantasy and a deep ambivalence towards powerful women. However, Marguerite de Valois carries a special interest for feminist historians, who paint a very different picture of her life as a whole. Best remembered for the massacre immediately following her ill-fated wedding, Valois' political interventions, support for the arts, and brilliance as a scholar and a writer tend to be forgotten. Born in 1553, Marguerite was only 19 at the time of her wedding; as mentioned above, after the massacre she campaigned actively with the Politiques to develop a policy of religious tolerance. Dubost notes that, despite the failure of this initiative, Marguerite's political role 'marks a new episode as a heroic act in a political role for women of the aristocracy'.[46]

Valois is also significant for her important cultural and intellectual achievements. Comparable in her intellectual accomplishments with her contemporary, the learned Elizabeth I of England, Marguerite was fluent in Italian, Spanish, Greek and, especially, Latin. She was extremely well read and took a leading role in fostering French arts and letters in the period bridging the late Renaissance and the baroque age. In her residences at Nérac and Usson, and later in Paris, Marguerite hosted theatrical events and welcomed poets and writers including Desportes, Malherbe, Régnier and de Viau – as well as Mainard, Racan and Gombauld, who would later be among the first members of the Académie Française.[47]

Using her royal position to facilitate the arts, Valois was also an accomplished poet, diarist and political analyst in her own right. Many of her letters have been preserved and published (notably correspondence with her husband Henri IV), along with poems attributed to her. From her vantage point in court and in the corridors of power, the princess published two essays of political and religious commentary: *Le Mémoire justificatif pour Henri de Bourbon* (1574) and *Discours docte et subtil* (1614). Best known among her writings is the three-volume *Mémoires*, first published posthumously in 1628 then reissued in many subsequent editions.[48] The *Mémoires* hold great historical importance as an insider's account of the tumultuous transitional years from the Valois dynasty to the Bourbons, including an eye-witness account of the massacre of Saint-Barthélemy. Notably, Valois' *Mémoires* describe a scene where the injured Protestant Lerac seeks refuge in her chambers ('his shirt soaked in blood') during the massacre and is spared by the captain of the guards due to Valois' compassion.[49] Dumas' novel and, in turn, its cinematic adaptations incorporate this episode in a boudoir account of the massacre, where Valois' lover La Môle is substituted for Lerac.

For feminist historian Viennot, Valois' ongoing popularity and historical significance arise centrally from her writings, through which her singular voice has been heard across the centuries.[50] Viennot's project is to bring to light the breadth and depth of Valois' life achievements, which are often forgotten and distorted by the persistent pornographic and inflammatory myths. This historian argues that the two inflammatory political pamphlets of 1574 noted above not only attacked Médicis but also launched the 'legend' of her youngest daughter. It was at this time that Valois was framed as a promiscuous young woman whose extensive list of purported lovers included her brothers.[51] A subsequent anonymously authored pamphlet of 1607, the influential *Le Divorce satyrique*, extends this depraved portrait.

Published after the marriage between Henri IV and Marie de Médicis, this tract sought to undermine the authority of Henri IV through a pornographic account of his first wife. *Le Divorce satyrique* painted a damaging picture of Henri IV (crowned king of France since 1593) as a cuckold, whose wife had bedded not only all the influential Huguenots but also virtually the entire court, as well as soldiers, servants, cooks and so on.[52] Viennot cites this pamphlet as the most vicious of many highly sexualised and distorted portraits of Valois. Largely absent in Dumas, this pornographic account recurs in Chéreau's film – notably in the scene where the masked princess and her friend Henriette de Nevers roam the streets of Paris on her wedding night seeking sex with strangers.

If the orgies of *Le Divorce satyrique* are clearly still points of reference in 1994, the mythology surrounding 'la reine Margot' developed more fully in the Romantic period as part of a broader fascination with powerful historical female figures. As mentioned above, this 18th-century fascination with the *Ancien Régime* in France was prompted in part by the tremendous upheaval of the Revolution. The Romantic period also coincided with the first feminist presence in France, 'provoking the development of a major controversy surrounding the balance of political power and now, throughout the century, a particular interest in women's history'.[53] Notably, during this period several new editions of Valois' *Mémoires* were issued by the major publishers of the genre. Finally, in 1844, Dumas' novel *La Reine Margot* – an inventive mixture of historical account and Romantic dramatic narrative – transformed the Renaissance legend into a veritable popular myth. By 1845, thanks to Dumas' novel, Valois had become the nation's most popular princess.[54]

Viennot, like Dubost, uses the term 'myth' to describe the multiple popular discourses surrounding Valois. The transformation of this historical figure into the larger than life 'reine Margot' exemplifies what Roland Barthes calls 'mythology'. In his 1957 work *Mythologies*, Barthes demonstrates how diverse phenomena from French popular culture (wrestling, the face of Garbo, travel guides and advertising images) have contributed to 'mythological' systems of meaning. For Barthes, myth forms a second order semiological system that builds upon linguistic structures of meaning. Briefly, a linguistic sign is the composite of a signifier (an image, a written or spoken word) and a signified (the mental image or concept suggested by that word or image). On this account, the linguistic signifier 'Marguerite de Valois' corresponds to the signified of a Renaissance princess (second daughter of Catherine de Médicis and Henri II, brother of Charles IX and wife of Henri IV, and so on). On the first order of signification, the sign 'Marguerite de Valois' is the 'associative total'[55] of this concept and its image/name.

The process of myth-making – the shift from 'Marguerite de Valois' to 'la reine Margot' – fixes specific historical meanings as 'natural'. As a 'type of speech chosen by history', myth carries greater, 'larger than life' cultural meanings with ideological weight. Like the linguistic sign, myth has a tripartite structure. The mythological signifier is a form, often a linguistic utterance or an image, where 'the meaning is *already* complete, it postulates a kind of knowledge, a past, a memory, a comparative order of facts, ideas, decisions'.[56] The mythological signifier is a concept, an accumulation of historically and culturally specific associations. Spatially and temporally specific yet empty in itself, the form is 'filled' by a range of intertextual knowledges.

For Barthes, form works through place and proximity. The abstract form – the face and body of contemporary actress Adjani as 'Margot' –

produces a psychic and cultural 'proximity' for the viewer through cinematic identification and intertextual references to Adjani's star persona. Meanwhile, the 'concept' (or cultural meaning) of this form attaches a condensation of vague, associative knowledges to the form. Importantly, for Barthes, these intertextual knowledges are 'memorial' in nature. Often associated with 'ideological' discourse, myth tends to work with familiar 'historical' and 'national' signifiers, rendering them 'natural' within a specific context. One of the greatest French myths is the figure of 'Marianne', the legendary heroine of the revolution who is featured most famously holding the French flag in Delacroix's Romantic painting *Les Trois Glorieuses Liberty Leading the People* (1830).

As a symbol of the French Republic, 'Marianne' continues to circulate widely within contemporary culture, where stars Brigitte Bardot and Catherine Deneuve have both been sculpted in this role. In this respect, this mythic figure is now routinely articulated with star images and other popular culture references.[57] I would argue that part of the mythological resonance of Adjani's 'Margot' draws from a reference to 'Marianne' in the film's striking cinematic projection of the figure of a young, white, beautiful woman within a violent tableau of French history. In this way, Chéreau's film draws selectively from a wide array of cultural discourses (including Jeanne Moreau's portrayal of Margot in Dréville's 1954 adaptation) in order to crystallise another fully 'mythic' portrait of 'la reine Margot' in 1994.

In the four centuries since Valois' death this historical figure has enjoyed many historical revivals, from the passion of the Romantics for Renaissance princesses to a renewed feminist interest from the 1880s to the First World War.[58] For Viennot, these waves of popularity often correspond to periods of strong feminist presence in France and related interest in important historical female figures. From the 1980s Viennot notes another heightened interest in Valois – an interest that was crystallised and amplified by the release of Chéreau's epic film. As I will discuss in Chapter 3, the release of *La Reine Margot* corresponded with a flurry of publications, including commentaries on the events surrounding the massacre, biographies of Valois and new editions of Dumas' novel.

If myth operates powerfully in the realm of the memorial, there is undoubtedly something intrinsically 'mythic' in the nature of contemporary French super-productions. Films such as *Cyrano de Bergerac, Les Misérables,*

*Le Colonel Chabert, La Reine Margot, Germinal, Lucie Aubrac* or *Jeanne d'Arc* intervene deliberately within the mythic realm of national archetypes. The cultural resonance of *La Reine Margot* arises from three interconnected elements that are in themselves 'mythic'. Firstly, the film's dramatisation of the terrible sectarian violence of the massacre of Saint-Barthélemy activates a series of discourses concerning nation, religious difference, power and violence. Secondly, the myth of historical narratives shaped through male virtuoso 'authorship' is filtered through the figures of Dumas and in turn Chéreau. Thirdly, the film's superimposition of the iconic historical figure of Margot with the mysterious and glamorous Adjani is absolutely pivotal to the film's cultural resonance in contemporary France.

### Adjani's 'Margot': the elusive superstar

The casting of French superstar Adjani is crucial to the film's vivid mythologisation of 'la reine Margot'. Chéreau remarks in an interview that *La Reine Margot* probably would not have been made without Adjani,

The Marianne mythology: Delacroix's Romantic painting *Les Trois Glorieuses Liberty Leading the People* (1830)

because at the moment of the film's production 'the dream of the French was for Isabelle to become part of the legend of "la reine Margot".'[59] As with Gérard Depardieu's performances of Cyrano de Bergerac, Colonel Chabert and Jean Valjean, the fusion of the French star with iconic literary and historical personas is essential to the cultural and industrial logic of recent super-productions. The role of Margot was written for Adjani, and her portrayal of the Renaissance princess is vital to the film's industrial profile and to its cultural meanings.

A major French film star since the 1970s, Adjani's elusive star persona and her reputation for emotionally charged performances contributed to the anticipation of a dramatic cinematic 'event' with the release of *La Reine Margot*. Adjani's star profile centres on her face, a flawless white oval with regular features and a small but full mouth. Also key to Adjani's ethereal beauty are her startlingly azure-blue eyes, which project a tremendous intensity belying the almost doll-like perfection of her features. Adjani's lush jet-black hair contrasts strikingly with the 'porcelain' whiteness of her face, which has often been characterised as a mask. A blank 'mask-like' remoteness of expression contrasts with a volatile expressiveness of face, voice and body, where the perfect white cameo of the face is disfigured in rage, passion or madness.

Born in 1955 to a German mother and an Algerian father, Adjani made her film debut at the age of 14 in *Le Petit bougnat* (1969). As a teenager she developed her acting skills in the theatre, including her acclaimed role as Agnes in Molière's *L'École des femmes* and Giraudoux's *Ondine* at the Comédie-Française (both in 1974). Adjani's first major film role also came in 1974 with *La Gifle*, in which she played the free-spirited daughter of divorced parents. Like many French film actors, Adjani has worked extensively in the theatre,[60] and this experience is brought to bear as part of a heightened 'theatrical' performance style.

The youngest member of the Comédie-Française at the age of 16, Adjani was reputedly 'poached' by François Truffaut to star in *L'Histoire d'Adèle H.* (1975).[61] This film, which fully launched Adjani's film career, chronicles the tragic fate of Adèle, the daughter of Victor Hugo, who is consumed by an unrequited passion. Obsessed to the point of violence, Adèle follows her lover first to Nova Scotia then to the West Indies. Gradually losing her mind, she is recognised and brought back to France, living out her days in a private sanatorium. According to Agnès Peck, this film inaugurates 'the face of Adjani as cinematic icon, site of resonance, figure of destiny'.[62] Adjani's face is the obsessive focus of Truffaut's portrait of the psychological and emotional dissolution of a beautiful and talented young woman (Hugo's daughter, Adèle is also a gifted writer in her own right).

The role in *L'Histoire d'Adèle H.* earned Adjani instant critical accolades and an Oscar nomination. Subsequently the actress appeared in a series of psychologically disturbed, sexually charged roles in auteurist works, including André Téchiné's *Barocco* (1976), Werner Herzog's *Nosferatu, Fantôme de la nuit/Nosferatu the Vampire* (1978) and Andrzej Zulawski's *Possession* (1980). In these films Adjani developed an intensive, naturalist and fully corporeal performance style, conveying unbridled passions and emotions. (For a full Adjani filmography see Appendix 3.) Adjani's early career culminates in a César award for *L'Été meurtrier* and César and Cannes awards for best actress in Zulawski's *Possession*.

Adjani's biggest popular hit came in 1982 with Jean Becker's psychological thriller *L'Été meurtrier/One Deadly Summer*. Here, she once again plays a psychologically disturbed seductress – a young woman obsessed with her mother's gang rape that resulted in her conception. With her great beauty and pornographic tales of sexual exploits, Adjani's character is known only as 'Elle' (the generic female pronoun 'She'). Elle holds a hypnotic power over her naive young husband, eventually manipulating him to kill an innocent man – a misplaced act of vengeance that results in his incarceration and her own confinement to a mental asylum. Many of Adjani's roles combine these

Adjani's introduction as the mythic 'Margot'

elements of psychological and sexual pathology in bravura performances that involve the dramatic dissolution from the perfect mask-like face and model's body into complete physical and psychological breakdown resulting in death or incarceration.

In the early 1980s Adjani added several popular films to her filmography, including comedies such as *Clara et les chics types* (1980) and *Tout feu tout flamme* (1981) – as well as two 1982 thrillers *L'Été meurtrier* and *Mortelle randonnée*. Since the 1970s Adjani has also developed a modest international profile with *Driver* (1977) with Ryan O'Neal, a role that put her on the cover of *Time* magazine; in 1980 she returned to costume film with James Ivory's *Quartet*. Like other French actresses, Adjani established a parallel career as a Dior model and advertising icon (the star was featured in advertising campaigns for Lux soap, Woolite detergent, Renault, Lejaby, and GAP socks in the United States).[63] Like other French female stars Catherine Deneuve, Juliette Binoche, Sophie Marceau, Emmanuelle Béart, Carole Bouquet and Vanessa Paradis, Adjani is an inter/national signifier of French luxury.[64]

A glamorous and critically acclaimed actress whose work spans both auteurist and popular films, Adjani was established as one of the major French female stars by the early 1980s. Yet, strangely, her subsequent career has been characterised largely by absence. The star's film roles have been rare and uneven, and her famous abhorrence of publicity has mostly kept her out of the public eye. Adjani's absence from public life has produced an aura of mystique, but it has also led to bizarre rumours: in 1986 Adjani was dogged by persistent gossip that she was suffering from AIDS; in January 1987 the star was forced to make a television appearance to refute these rumours after the tabloid press reported that she had died from the disease.

Critics and Adjani herself suggest that these rumours were linked to the star's declaration of her German and Algerian roots. In the context of increasing racism associated with the rise of the extreme right-wing National Front, Adjani's public stand compromised her favoured position as a luminous symbol of perfect French femininity. For Richard Dyer, part of the preciousness of the female star is precisely her *whiteness*, where she becomes 'a light source', 'shining', 'golden' and 'glittering'; indeed, a crucial part of Adjani's star image is the gleaming white oval of her face. Guy Austin argues that, with the revelation of her Algerian roots, Adjani's iconic

French 'whiteness' was tainted by the tensions arising in the wake of the 1954–1962 Algerian War – 'the source during the 1980s of demonstrations and debates on issues such as war crimes, torture and rights for Algerian immigrants'.[65]

After the AIDS episode, controversies over the star's identity were fuelled by her high-profile appearances in a demonstration with the SOS Racisme movement and in Algeria, where she spoke out against torture in 1988. Finally, when receiving her César award for *Camille Claudel* she read a passage from Salman Rushdie's *Satanic Verses* to denounce the persecution of artists.[66] During this period Adjani consistently aligned herself with the oppressed; this aspect of her star image informs Adjani's role in *La Reine Margot*, where the young queen defends the endangered Huguenots against the Catholic oppressors. Another aspect of Adjani's star persona, her rumoured association with illness, arises in the protagonist's insanity in *Camille Claudel* – and, as I will elaborate in the next chapter, in *La Reine Margot*'s powerful images of blood and death. Adjani comments lucidly: 'The enemy is the "sick woman". And it's still always reassuring for society that disease should strike those living at the margins, labelled and excluded by the social and moral order: Marguerite, prostitutes, homosexuals, drug users, blacks, artists, women.'[67]

During a period when she made few films, Adjani's private life was the subject of extensive speculation in the popular press. Linked romantically with cameraman and director Bruno Nuytten, as well as actors Warren Beatty and Daniel Day-Lewis, the actress is the mother of two sons: Barnabé (with Nuytten) and Gabriel Kane (with Day-Lewis). Her relationship with Day-Lewis was reported to be particularly tempestuous, and their protracted break-up fuelled a flurry of unwelcome publicity. Famously hostile to this type of media attention, Adjani gained a reputation for being difficult and capricious. During this period the star stated publicly that her highly selective choice of appearances was necessary to preserve her artistic integrity.

Describing Adjani's unusual star status as 'postmodern', Jean-Marc Lalanne suggests that after *L'Été meurtrier* the French national cinema was too narrow to accommodate her growing mythological status. Instead of the character-driven leading roles still played by Catherine Deneuve and Juliette Binoche, Adjani's star image fractured into a simulacrum of the cinema: glamour photos, clips and an image of inaccessibility. 'With Adjani, for the first time, the remoteness inherent in the star status is extended into a distancing of cinema itself.'[68] Lalanne cites the narcissistic and schizophrenic dissolution of the actress in a field of images and mirrors in *Mortelle randonnée*, and Adjani's bizarre cameos in *Subway*, where she appears at odd intervals like a fashion model, wearing a new outfit each time.

Adjani's next major role was in Bruno Nuytten's 1987 *Camille Claudel*, where she plays a talented young sculptress engaged in a damaging relationship with master sculptor Rodin (Gérard Depardieu). Following Lalanne, it could be argued that, in *Camille Claudel* and *La Reine Margot*, Adjani's larger than life star presence is matched by the mythic quality of the roles and the epic scale of the films. In *Camille Claudel*, Adjani's passionate sculptress faces off with Depardieu's Rodin in love and art. Nuytten's film charts the brilliance and decline of the real historical figure, Rodin's student, muse and lover, whose own talent was subsumed by the male sculptor's fame and ego. In keeping with earlier roles, the actress depicts Claudel's descent into madness with complete physical and emotional abandon. This role is strongly reminiscent of Adjani's character in *L'Histoire d'Adèle H.*, but it is important to note that the star was the major architect of *Camille Claudel*, being credited as producer and star. A clear precursor to her later period role as 'Margot', Adjani's performance garnered her a third César as well as an Oscar nomination for best actress.

In the decade leading up to *La Reine Margot*, Adjani appeared only in Luc Besson's *Subway* (1984), *Camille Claudel* and two minor films, *Ishtar* (1985) and *Toxic Affair* (1993). Playing up the elusive star's imminent appearance, the considerable advance publicity for *La Reine Margot* worked to set up the mythic cinematic 'event' – Adjani as 'Margot' – long before the film was released. As I will elaborate in Chapter 3, Adjani's face and body in period costume are foregrounded to produce a visual amalgamation of star and mythic historical figure. François Jonquet has described this process in *Globe hebdo*:

> All at once, the great media machine pulls out all the stops. It generates mythology with a vengeance and plays on the good old equation that backs up the invention of the star: Through her status and her personal history, Adjani IS queen Margot, often humiliated (think of the disastrous box office of *Toxic Affair*), secretive, monstrous, elated, concerned for the 'side of the oppressed' as is said of her with reference to the clumsy concerns of the present.[69]

In the film's pre-release publicity, Adjani's choice of role figures centrally. Interviews with scriptwriter Thompson and Chéreau recount how they persuaded Adjani to come out of seclusion for this film. Adjani herself comments that she chose this role in order to work with Chéreau, taking up the 'chance to tackle a legendary French historical figure in a very modern manner. With a director who has his vigour and his experience, one is tempted to take risks.'[70] Notably, Adjani's rationale for playing Margot turns on the 'risks' associated with auteur cinema.

Billed prominently as a star vehicle for Adjani, *La Reine Margot* is also promoted as Chéreau's auteurist project in which the star heads up a cast of esteemed actors, including Daniel Auteuil (Navarre), Jean-Hugues Anglade (Charles IX), Vincent Perez (La Môle), Pascal Greggory (Anjou), Dominique Blanc (Henriette) and Miguel Bosè (Guise). The casting of Perez as La Môle follows from his period film track record, notably as Roxanne's lover Christian in *Cyrano de Bergerac* and as romantic lead in *Indochine*. Meanwhile, the casting of veteran Daniel Auteuil (*Jean de Florette* (1986), *Manon des Sources* (1986), *Un coeur en hiver* (1992)) infuses Navarre with a humanity beyond Perez as the handsome but doomed lover. Further, Italian actress Virna Lisi (*La Tulipe noire* (1965), *Signore e Signori* (1965)) offers a brilliant performance as the sinister Médicis.

The film's narrative image of the Valois family as a 'monstrous clan' is enabled by this international all-star ensemble cast in bravura performances. For Adjani and the other actors, *La Reine Margot* is billed as an actor's film under the direction of eminent theatre auteur Chéreau. Notably, Anglade, Perez, Greggory and Blanc had previously collaborated with Chéreau on film and in the theatre.[71] Ultimately, the film's most startling performance comes from the boyish, baby-faced Anglade, associated with the superficial 1980s 'cinema du look' (*Subway*, *37°2 le matin/Betty Blue* (1985), *La Femme Nikita* (1989)).[72] In *La Reine Margot*, Anglade is transformed into an alternately charming and vicious king Charles IX, whose death from poison transpires in an operatic scene, writhing in agony and sweating blood.

## Genre and industrial cycles: French costume film

As a historical epic with an all-star international cast, *La Reine Margot* is typical of a cycle of French 'super-productions' released in the late 1980s and early to mid-1990s. Produced with an eye to national and international audiences alike, these spectacular 'media events' emerge from a particular conjuncture of the French film industry. This industrial context and the critical debates specific to French historical cinema arise from the long-standing, and sometimes controversial, traditions of 'quality' film production.

Historians of French cinema have noted the importance of literary adaptations and historical films as markers of a prestigious national cultural heritage.[73] This trend began in the silent era of French cinema with multiple silent versions of Hugo's and Dumas' works, and continued into the sound era, when, for instance, Hugo's Romantic hero Jean Valjean is immortalised by Harry Baur in the moody 1933 Les Misérables, and again in 1957 by Jean Gabin. In industrial terms, 'costume' (le film en costume), 'historical' or 'swashbuckling' (films de cape et d'épée) styles have historically enjoyed great popularity, both within France and as cultural exports.[74] For Pierre Guibbert, the swashbuckling film is a quintessential French genre, holding an iconic place in the popular imagination comparable to the American Western, the British period drama or the Italian peplum film.[75]

The swashbuckling film arises directly from the Romantic literary tradition, adapting works by Dumas (Les Trois Mousquetaires/The Three Musketeers), Le Masque de fer/The Man in the Iron Mask, La Dame de Montsoreau and La Reine Margot), Hugo (Les Misérables, The Hunchback of Notre Dame), Edmond Rostand (Cyrano de Bergerac), Théophile Gautier (La Capitaine Fracasse), Michel Zévaco (the Pardaillan series, Le Capitan) and Paul Féval (Le Bossu).[76] From the first years of silent cinema, these classics have inspired multiple adaptations in every decade of French cinema; examples include Les Mousquetaires de la reine by Georges Méliès in 1903, Max Linder's 1922 L'Étroit mousquetaire, Abel Gance's 1940 Le Capitaine Fracasse and Christian-Jaque's 1952 Fanfan la tulipe. More recent productions in this tradition include Rappeneau's Cyrano de Bergerac and Philippe de Broca's 1997 Le Bossu.

One of the great pleasures of the genre is the play of repetition and difference across the different historical eras, cinematic styles and performances. Different film, theatre and television versions of classic tales or performances of 'mythic' personas do not exhaust the cultural significance of these works but, rather, regenerate them across time. Prior to Chéreau's project, La Reine Margot has been adapted twice for the screen:

an early television version by Louis Chavance (1961) and Dréville's 1954 film. As prestigious productions of their respective eras, Chéreau's and Dréville's adaptations each contribute richly to the myth of Margot. Crucial to the pleasures of costume and swashbuckling films is the memory play between different screen versions of the myth – Adjani's Margot in an intertextual shadowplay with Jeanne Moreau in the same role 40 years earlier.

Filmed at the height of a post-war cycle of French costume films, Dréville's 1954 version encapsulates the elaborate studio style of the period; elements of this style include the star system, constructed sets, sophisticated lighting, sharp dialogue, a return to literary sources and showy filming techniques including complex camera movements.[77] Scripted by Abel Gance (*Napoléon* (1927/1934)), the film features a studio construction of the Louvre exterior on the banks of the Seine and handsome interiors. As part of a 1950s spectacle of popular entertainment, Dréville's film features several elaborate set pieces: the procession of Margot and Navarre in court after their wedding, the wedding dance, extended fencing scenes – and a theatrical staging of the massacre. As I will discuss in Chapter 2, the crepuscular atmosphere and graphic violence of Chéreau's film differentiates it from the 1950s costume film tradition exemplified by Dréville's film.

Following the studio style of the period, Dréville favours long shots and medium shots rather than close-ups, and Moreau's Margot is primarily framed in medium and long shots. Moreau's elaborate gowns (by Rosine

Dréville's 1954 *La Reine Margot* featuring Françoise Rosay as the odious Médicis (foreground) and Jeanne Moreau as 'Margot'

Delamare), careful make-up and hairstyles render her a remote, statuesque, almost untouchable figure, contrasting strongly with the dramatic close-ups and the dishevelled appearance of Adjani (and the other actors) in the 1994 version. However, we can also trace thematic continuities between the two films. Moreau's ornamental role and Françoise Rosay's scheming, witch-like Médicis are consonant with a problematic framing of powerful historical women within 1950s French costume film. For Geneviève Sellier, Dumas' devalorisation of powerful female figures is accentuated in Dréville's film.

> This inflection is typical of the genre of the period, at the time of the box office triumph of Sacha Guitry's *Si Versailles m'était conté*. The devalorisation of the feminine in the 1950s, a period marked by a 'return to the patriarchal order', is often achieved through a reduction of young women to sexual objects and the derisory treatment of older women.[78]

Dréville's *La Reine Margot* belongs to a post-war return to 'quality' literary adaptation and costume films within the French film industry. At a time when the French market was inundated with previously unreleased American films, the 'tradition of quality' took on new cultural and economic significance. From the late 1940s French filmmakers undertook capital-intensive American-style productions featuring popular stars, elaborate sets and costumes. This era is best characterised by Renoir's *French Cancan* (1955), and by the works of 1950s French stars Martine Carol (*Caroline chérie* (1951) and *Nana* (1955)) and Gérard Philipe (*Les Grandes manoeuvres* (1955) and *Fanfan la tulipe*). Alan Williams notes how these films were produced partly as a nationalistic cultural strategy,[79] functioning as they would again in the 1980s and 1990s as an 'official' state-approved form of cinema.

The 1950s marked the pinnacle of film as popular entertainment in France, and from 1958 cinema attendance went into decline with the rise of television.[80] In the 1960s historical fiction as a popular genre was eclipsed at the box office by the *policier* genre. Meanwhile, the 'feminine' popular genre of historical fiction was critically disparaged by advocates of the emergent French new wave. For instance, in his 1954 auteurist manifesto 'A certain tendency of the French cinema', François Truffaut famously critiqued what he called the 'tradition of quality'. Singling out the dominance of what he called the 'metteurs-en-scène' and a slavish over-reliance on the classic French novel, he remarked caustically that 'a film is no longer made in France that the authors do not believe they are re-making Madame Bovary'.[81]

Lambasting bourgeois popular cinema in the name of auteurist production, Truffaut spoke for a new generation of filmmakers who rejected what they saw as a backward-looking French cultural tradition. From a decline in the 1960s, the 1970s and early 1980s saw the sporadic production of prestigious historical films such as *Stavisky* (1974), *L'Histoire d'Adèle H.*, *Le Dernier métro/The Last Metro* (1980) and *Danton* (1982). However, it was Claude Berri's 1986 adaptations of Pagnol's *Jean de Florette* and *Manon des Sources* that signalled a renewed cultural and commercial viability for French literary adaptation.

Other major historical productions of the 1980s included Tavernier's *Un Dimanche à la campagne* (1984) and *La Vie et rien d'autre* (1989) and Schlöndorff's Proust homage *Un Amour de Swann/Swann in Love* (1983), and Yves Robert's 1990 Pagnol adaptations *La Gloire de mon père* and *Le Château de ma mère*. These productions coincided with the rise of British 'heritage' films such as *Chariots of Fire* (1981), *Gandhi* (1982) and *A Room with a View* (1986). Like the British heritage films, the 1980s French heritage films are 'imbued with nostalgia for the golden age of the cinema, as well as the golden age of a rural France untainted by rapid post-war industrialisation and the alienation of increasing urbanisation in the 1980s and 1990s'.[82] Surprise hits not only in France but also in the coveted international market, Berri's pastoral works undoubtedly helped precipitate later big-budget productions such as *Camille Claudel* in 1987 and, especially, Rappeneau's 1989 *Cyrano de Bergerac*.

*Cyrano* became the top-grossing French film, earning some FF60,000,000 in the domestic market, and more than FF50,000,000 abroad.[83] For Keith Reader, it is 'the Cyrano phenomenon' that ushers in a new mode of French cinema for British (and other international) audiences. In contrast with an auteurist tradition, Reader points to 'films whose "Frenchness" plays a much more significant part in their appeal'.[84] Noting the unprecedented popularity of the lavish production values and big-screen adaptations for English audiences, this critic foregrounds the appeal of 'the epic quality that makes … an ideal vehicle for the "night-out" brand of cinemagoing that has become increasingly important since the spread of video'.[85] In fact, in the early 1990s period films were counted among the most profitable French film exports: *Cyrano*, *Valmont* (1989) and *L'Amant* each earned more than FF50,000,000 on the international market, while *Camille Claudel* earned more than FF10,000,000.[86]

*Cyrano's* success inspired a revival of French 'quality' historical fiction in the early 1990s with projects such as *Madame Bovary* (1991), *Tous les matins du monde* (1992), *L'Amant, Indochine, Germinal* and *La Fille d'Artagnan* (1994). As we shall see in the Conclusion, this mode of production continued into the late 1990s and early 2000s. Taken together, this prolific cycle of French historical productions and literary adaptations incorporates smaller projects (such as *Ridicule* (1996) or *Les Enfants du Siècle* (1999)) as well as television films and mini-series – and a select group of 'super-productions' that project the features of the minor productions onto a more epic and mythic scale of cinematic 'event'.

Like the 1950s 'tradition of quality', recent French period films incorporate historical settings, literary sources and the all-important high production values and star codes. The award-winning *La Reine Margot* follows this formula as an epic Dumas adaptation with an all-star international cast. Recent French super-productions recall Truffaut's 1954 critique of the formulaic, prestigious and artistically unambitious 'quality' productions. This disparaging attitude towards costume film continues in specialist film journals such as *Cahiers du cinéma*. Yet, as I will discuss in Chapter 3, *La Reine Margot* was billed as epic popular entertainment with the added value of an auteurist work.

In part, Truffaut's 1950s critique claimed that state-sanctioned 'quality' projects stifled the French film industry. Issues surrounding state sponsorship and cultural policy recur in subsequent debates. Begun in the post-war period,[87] state support for film production was increased as a matter of government policy in the 1980s. Jack Lang, President Mitterrand's Minister of Culture, established a tax shelter for film financing, and doubled the existing subsidy of *avance sur recettes*. Originally instituted in 1960, this policy provided selective financing to target films judged by the allocation commission to be 'quality' productions. There was considerable controversy surrounding the selection process, where the term 'quality' could mean works by established directors, innovative films by new talents, or large-scale super-productions such as *Germinal* and *La Reine Margot*.[88] Lang's policies promoted a new kind of French 'quality', the filming of France's historical and cultural past as a form of national education, aiming to incite 'the return of the general public to the cinema'.[89]

Claude Berri's 1993 production *Germinal* most directly embodies the pedagogical cultural policy of the period. Billed as the most expensive French film production ever, the budget of *Germinal* was FF173 million,[90] with a huge cast headed by Depardieu, Miou-Miou and the singer Renaud. Based on Émile Zola's novel, *Germinal* depicts the exploitation of the miners of the north of France in the latter part of the 19th century. *Germinal* is explicitly framed as a leftist–nationalist project. The director notes in an interview that the film could have been shot more cheaply in Poland or Hungary, but that the filmmakers opted to shoot in the novel's French region of Nord-Pas-de-Calais, casting unemployed local workers as extras. There was some controversy around the state-sponsored *Germinal* adaptation considering that the region's mines had recently ceased operations; as a result, the filmmakers had to reconstruct a mine shaft at Paillancourt.[91]

*Germinal* marks an important point of reference for *La Reine Margot*. Based on classic French novels, both films depict historical milieux with the support of the *avance sur recettes* subsidy. Berri's epic was released in September 1993 and Chéreau's film followed seven months later in May 1994, and both were significant media events in France. Like *Cyrano de Bergerac*, *Germinal* and *La Reine Margot* were conceived, financed and marketed through star players associated with iconic literary roles and large-scale productions. Although, as we will see in Chapter 3 the critical response to the two projects varied, these two works exemplify the spectacular 'economy of scale' that became increasingly important for the French film industry from the 1980s.

In order to compete with the American blockbusters dominating the French market, René Prédal notes that, since the 1980s, certain French producers have sought to address international audiences through spectacular productions, the star system and 'media events'.[92] This critic traces the tendency back to Roman Polanski's 1979 *Tess* and Jean-Jacques Annaud's 1981 *La Guerre du feu/ Quest for Fire*. In these films, as well as his later works such as *Nom de la rose/ The Name of the Rose* (1986) and *L'Ours/The Bear* (1989), Annaud laboured for three or four years on each project, generating great anticipation for the film's eventual release. For instance, in adapting Umberto Eco's prestigious medieval novel *The Name of the Rose*,

Annaud publicised the 'film of films' through an elaborate and expensive production process featuring original sets at Cinecittà, and a cast starring Sean Connery, F. Murray Abraham and Christian Slater (along with hundreds of extras).[93]

Following Annaud's success, this logic of production and publicity was subsequently adopted for *Camille Claudel, Cyrano de Bergerac, Le Colonel Chabert, Germinal, La Reine Margot, Le Hussard sur le toit* and *Jeanne d'Arc*. Frequently receiving support through state sponsorship and publicised as prestige French products, these projects also rely upon long-standing practices of television co-financing and international co-productions. *Germinal*, for example, was a French/Italian project, while *La Reine Margot* was a French, Italian and German co-production. With a budget of FF140 million,[94] the film was produced by Claude Berri's Renn Productions, co-produced by the television company France 2 Cinéma, D.A. Films, the Italian company R.C.S. Films and TV and the German Nef Filmproduktion.[95]

As producer on *La Reine Margot*, writer/director Claude Berri was central to the 'super-production' trend. Berri was credited as writer/director on the influential Pagnol adaptations *Jean de Florette* and *Manon des Sources*, as he was on *Germinal* and *Lucie Aubrac*. He has been perhaps even more influential for this cycle of huge-scale projects as producer on *Tess, L'Ours, L'Amant, Germinal* and the two *Astérix et Obélix* films (1999/2002). Berri brought to *La Reine Margot* a proven track record of financing and marketing epic films, and his participation was crucial to a project of this scale and ambition. In addition to its high-profile cast, director and producer, *La Reine Margot* can boast a prestigious international production team. Within a publicity campaign foregrounding the singular marks of authorship, Danièle Thompson (*Cousin Cousine* (1975), *La Boum* (1980)) was credited as the lead scriptwriter.

The film was shot by award-winning cinematographer Philippe Rousselot (*Diva* (1980), *L'Ours, Trop belle pour toi* (1988), *Dangerous Liaisons* (1988), *A River Runs Through It* (1989), *Interview with the Vampire* (1993–1994)). In keeping with the genre's promise of stunning period locations, *La Reine Margot* was shot on location at several European sites. Although the script called for Notre Dame de Paris for the wedding scene, permission proved difficult, and the scene was eventually shot in the Saint-Quentin basilica.[96] The action at the Louvre was shot partly in reconstructed sets at the Théâtre de Nanterre and on location in Portugal at the National Palace of Mafra. The street scenes of the massacre were shot in Bordeaux (standing in for the streets of Paris), while the hunt sequence was filmed in the forests of Rambouillet.

The film also boasts an original score by Serbo-Croatian composer Goran Bregovic, who has worked extensively with Serbian director Emir Kusturica on *Arizona Dream* (1991) and *Underground* (1995). Bregovic's film scores are conceived as semi-independent musical projects, and his soundtrack of 'Arizona Dream' (with Iggy Pop) became a certified Gold Record. Moidele Bickel, who won the César award for best costume design, has worked extensively in the theatre (including Chéreau's 1992 production of Berg's opera *Wozzeck*). Head production designer Richard Peduzzi is another of Chéreau's theatrical collaborators, and production designer Olivier Radot worked on *L'Amant* and *Germinal*. These veteran crew members, alongside the all-star cast and romantic period settings, contribute to the film's profile as a prestigious super-production.

In the next chapter, I will examine in further detail how the film incorporates the elements of the super-production to deliver a visceral and dynamic period spectacle, while in some ways confounding the audience's expectations of the genre.

## Notes

References to some daily press reviews from the Bibliothèque du film do not have page numbers; these can be found at the Bibliothèque du film, 100, rue du Faubourg Saint-Antoine, 75012 Paris, France.

All translations from the French are mine, unless an English-language source is indicated.

1   All references in this guide are to the well-known writer Alexandre Dumas 'père' (1802–1870), rather than his son, usually designated as Alexandre Dumas 'fils'.

2   The European Counter-Reformation is generally regarded as beginning with the 1545 Council of Trent, at which the Roman Catholic Church officially reinstated the totality of Catholic dogma in response to Protestant reforms introduced by Luther and Calvin. As a result, those practising the 'heretical' new religion were widely persecuted from the mid-16th century. For instance, in 1555 Pope Paul IV revived the Inquisition, which was at its most violent in

Italy and Spain. See Goubert, Pierre, *The Course of French History* (London, 1984), pp. 95–96.

3    Holt, Mack P., *The French Wars of Religion, 1562–1629* (Cambridge, 1995), p. 85.

4    See Crouzet, Denis, *La Nuit de la Saint-Barthélemy: Un rêve perdu de la Renaissance* (Paris, 1994), pp. 30–31.

5    See Sutherland, N.M., *The Massacre of Saint Bartholomew and the European Conflict 1559-1572* (London, 1973), pp. 1–19.

6    Ibid., pp. 4, 15.

7    Significantly, Philip II was married to Élisabeth de Valois, the eldest daughter of Henri II of France and Catherine de Médicis. See Appendix 2.

8    Sutherland, *The Massacre of Saint Bartholomew*, pp. 146–151.

9    La Môle's connection with the 'Netherlands Enterprise' can be traced back to July 1572, when he was sent by Charles IX as an envoy proposing Alençon's hand in marriage to Elizabeth I of England. This proposal was intended to secure an important alliance between the French Catholic monarchy and the English Protestant queen. Part of La Môle's mission was also, probably, to convince Elizabeth to declare war against Spain over the Protestant Netherlands uprising. Ibid., pp. 299–303.

10   Holt, *The French Wars of Religion*, pp. 77–78.

11   See Dubost, Jean-François, 'La Légende noire de la Reine Margot', *L'Histoire* 177 (1994), pp. 11–13.

12   See Sutherland, *The Massacre of Saint Bartholomew*, pp. 10–12, 344–346.

13   Holt, *The French Wars of Religion*, p. 87. For a more detailed account of the massacre, see Diefendorf, Barbara, *Beneath the Cross: Catholics and Huguenots in Sixteenth-Century Paris* (Oxford, 1991), pp. 93–106.

14   See Viennot, Éliane, *Marguerite de Valois: Histoire d'une femme, histoire d'un mythe* (Paris, 1993), pp. 65–71.

15   Dubost, 'La Légende noire de la Reine Margot', p. 13.

16   Goubert, *The Course of French History*, p. 104. For a useful overview of French political history between 1560 and 1610, see pp. 93–121.

17   Dubost, 'La Légende noire de la Reine Margot', p. 15.

18   Crouzet, *La Nuit de la Saint-Barthélemy*, p. 26.

19   For a full account of the French Protestant struggles of the 16th century, see Sutherland, N.M., *The Huguenot Struggle for Recognition* (New Haven, CT, 1980).

20   See Goubert, *The Course of French History*, pp. 132–133.

21   For a succinct discussion of the complex interplay between Church and state, see Reynolds, Siân, 'How the French present is shaped by the past: the last hundred years in historical perspective', in W. Kidd and S. Reynolds (eds), *Contemporary French Cultural Studies* (London, 2000), pp. 24–29.

22   On French Protestant 'sites of memory', see Joutard, Philippe, 'The museum of the desert: the Protestant minority', in P. Nora (ed.), *Realms of Memory: The Construction of the French Past* (New York, 1996), pp. 353–378.

23   See Reynolds, 'How the French present is shaped by the past', pp. 27–29.

24   This date recalls the events of 16-17 July 1942, when 13,000 French Jews were imprisoned for five days in the Vélodrome d'Hiver prior to deportation. See Kidd, William, 'Frenchness: constructed and reconstructed', in Kidd and Reynolds (eds), *Contemporary French Cultural Studies*, p. 160.

25   Vincendeau, Ginette, 'Unsettling memories', *Sight and Sound* (July 1995), p. 30.

26 Rosenstone, Robert A., 'The historical film as real history', *Film-Historia* 5/1 (1999), p. 18. Please note that the critical distinction discussed by Rosenstone does not reflect his own, much more nuanced position.

27 de la Bretèque, François, 'Le film en costumes: un bon objet?', *Cinémaction* 65 (1992), p. 121.

28 See Pidduck, Julianne, *Contemporary Costume Film: Space, Place and the Past* (London, 2005), Samuel, Raphael, *Theatres of Memory: Past and Present in Contemporary Culture* (London, 1994), de la Bretèque, 'Le film en costumes' and Landy, Marcia, *British Genres* (Princeton, 1991).

29 Nora, Pierre, 'From *Lieux de mémoire* to *Realms of Memory*', in Nora (ed.), *Realms of Memory*, p. xvii.

30 Nora, Pierre, 'Between memory and history', in Nora (ed.), *Realms of Memory*, p. 2.

31 For a general account of European Romanticism, see Porter, Roy and Teich, Mikulás' 'Introduction', in R. Porter and M. Teich (eds), *Romanticism in National Context* (Cambridge, 1988), pp. 1–36.

32 For a selective account of French Romanticism, see Bann, Stephen, 'Romanticism in France', in Porter and Teich (eds), *Romanticism in National Context*, pp. 240–259.

33 Ibid., p. 255.

34 Ibid., p. 256.

35 Aziza, Claude, 'Préface', in A. Dumas, *La Reine Margot* (Paris, 1994), p. 9.

36 See Viennot, *Marguerite de Valois*, p. 323.

37 In an interview, Chéreau specifically cites the influence of Géricault. See Caster, Sylvie, 'La reine magot', *Le Canard enchaîné*, 11 May 1994, p. 55.

38 See Vaughan, William, 'The visual arts', in D.G. Charlton (ed.), *The French Romantics* (Cambridge, 1984), p. 311.

39 Ibid., p. 312.

40 For an account of the Romantic vision of masculine creative genius, see Battersby, Christine, *Gender and Genius: Towards a Feminist Aesthetics* (Bloomington, IN, 1989), p. 156.

41 Toubiana, Serge, 'La Reine Margot: complot de famille', *Cahiers du cinéma* 479/80 (1994), pp. 9–11.

42 For an in-depth account of Chéreau's multifaceted career, see *Théâtre au cinéma: Patrice Chéreau, Jean Genet, Bernard-Marie Koltès* (Bobigny, 1999).

43 Chéreau, Patrice, 'Director's notes', *La Reine Margot* (English press book, 1994), p. 1.

44 Chéreau, 'Director's notes', p. 2.

45 See Viennot, *Marguerite de Valois*, pp. 237–238.

46 Dubost, 'La Légende noire de la Reine Margot', p. 14.

47 Ibid., p. 16.

48 For complete details on Marguerite de Valois' writings and their publications, see Viennot, *Marguerite de Valois*, pp. 451–454.

49 Written two decades after these events, Valois is undoubtedly careful to frame her role in the massacre in a favourable light; she also describes saving the life of future king Henri IV. For an account of the events surrounding the wedding and its fateful aftermath, see de Valois, Marguerite, *Mémoires et autres écrits de Marguerite de Valois, la reine Margot* (Paris, 1971), pp. 52–59.

50 Viennot, *Marguerite de Valois*, p. 12.

51    Ibid., p. 238.

52    Ibid., pp. 243–245.

53    Ibid., p. 314.

54    Ibid., p. 326.

55    Barthes, Roland, *Mythologies* (London, 1973), p. 114.

56    Ibid., p. 117.

57    See Vincendeau, Ginette, *Stars and Stardom in French Cinema* (London, 2000), pp. 36–37.

58    Viennot, *Marguerite de Valois*, pp. 355–362.

59    Cited in Macia, Jean-Luc, 'Margot dans l'ombre de Chéreau', *La Croix*, 12 May 1994.

60    Vincendeau notes the historical proximity between French stage and screen, where stars move fluidly between the two media. See her *Stars and Stardom*, pp. 2–10.

61    See Andrew, Geoff, 'Isabelle époque', *Time Out*, 11–18 January 1995, p. 26.

62    Peck, Agnès, 'Isabelle Adjani ombre et lumière', *Positif* 495 (2002), p. 26.

63    See the 'evene.fr' website: http://www.evene.fr/celebre/fiche.php?id_auteur=1822.

64    On the significance of French female stars as models, see Vincendeau, *Stars and Stardom*, pp. 35–38.

65    Austin, Guy, *Stars in Modern French Film* (London, 2003), p. 101.

66    Ibid., p. 24.

67    Adjani, cited in Austin, *Stars in Modern French Film*, p. 104.

68    Lalanne, Jean-Marc, 'Isabelle Adjani, en quelques états', *Le Mensuel du cinéma* 27 (1994), p. 70.

69    Jonquet, François, '*La Reine Margot* vaut-elle cette messe?', *Globe hebdo*, 11 May 1994, p. 34.

70    Cited in Pascal, Michel, 'Conversation à deux voix avec le couple Margot–Henri de Navarre', *Le Point* 1129, 7 May 1994, p. 103.

71    Chéreau's previous films featured Anglade and Greggory in *L'Homme blessé* and *Le Temps et le chambre*, respectively. Meanwhile, in the theatre Chéreau directed Perez (*Platonov* (1987) and *Hamlet* (1988)), Blanc (*Peer Gynt* (1981) and *Les Paravents* (1983)) and Greggory (*Hamlet*, and *Le Temps et la Chambre* (1991)). See *La Reine Margot* (English press book), pp. 19-27.

72    On the '*cinema du look*', see Austin, Guy, *Contemporary French Cinema: An Introduction* (Manchester, 1996), pp. 119–135.

73    See Hayward, Susan, *French National Cinema* (London, 1993), pp. 96-99 and Williams, Alan, *Republic of Images: A History of French Filmmaking* (Cambridge, 1992), pp. 277–281.

74    Prior to sound film, the swashbuckling films proved popular internationally, and this genre was borrowed in the United States, notably in the the films of Douglas Fairbanks and Errol Flynn. For analysis of this popular genre, see Desbarats, F., 'Autour de l'épée', *Cahiers de la cinémathèque* 51/52 (1989), pp. 73–88 and Guibbert, Pierre, 'Le film de cape et d'épée', *CinémAction* 68 (1993), pp. 154–159.

75    Guibbert, 'Le film de cape et d'épée', p. 155.

76    Ibid., p. 156.

77    Prédal, René, *Le Cinéma français depuis 1945* (Paris, 1991), p. 82.

78    Sellier, Geneviève, 'La Reine Margot au cinéma: Jean Dréville (1954) et Patrice Chéreau (1994)', in O. Krakovitch, G. Sellier and E. Viennot (eds), *Femmes de*

*pouvoir: Mythes et fantasmes* (Paris, 2001), p. 211. For an account of the 'return to the patriarchal order' in French post-war cinema, see Burch, Noël and Sellier, Geneviève, *La Drôle de guerre des sexes du cinéma français* (*1930–1956*) (Paris, 1996), pp. 245–277.

79  Williams, *Republic of Images*, pp. 278–279.

80  Prédal, *Le Cinéma français depuis 1945*, p. 68.

81  Truffaut, François, 'A certain tendency of the french cinema', in B. Nichols (ed.), *Movies and Methods* (Berkeley, 1976), p. 232.

82  Powrie, Phil and Reader, Keith, *French Cinema: A Student's Guide* (London, 2002), p. 39.

83  Condon, Anne Marie, 'Cinema', in S. Perry (ed.), *Aspects of Contemporary France* (London, 1997), p. 214.

84  Reader, Keith 'Le phénomène Cyrano: perceptions of French cinema in Britain', *Franco-British Studies* 15 (1993), p. 3.

85  Ibid., p. 8.

86  See 'Recettes d'exportation des quinze premiers films français à l'étranger', *Centre national de la cinématographie* 254 (1994), p. 8. It is worth noting that key films such as *Jean de Florette* and *Cyrano de Bergerac* continued to generate revenue long after their original release dates.

87  The practice of explicit government support for 'quality' productions was instituted in 1953, when significant state support amounting to approximately one-third of the production budget began to be awarded on the basis of the film's 'educational value' or its capacity for 'worldwide dissemination of the French language'. See Prédal, *Le Cinéma français depuis 1945*, p. 70.

88  See Hayward, *French National Cinema*, pp. 46–48.

89  See Austin, *Contemporary French Cinema*, p. 144.

90  de Gasquet, Pierre, 'Un test décisif pour les superproduction "à la française"', *Les Echos*, 29 September 1993.

91  'Cinéma-Germinal', Agence France Presse, 1 August 1992, p.1.

92  See Prédal, *Le Cinéma français depuis 1945*, p. 401.

93  Ibid., p. 409.

94  Lefevre, Raymond, 'Une autre vision de La Reine Margot', *Le Mensuel du cinéma* 17 (1994), p. 66.

95  'Les films de long métrage agréés au cours de l'année 1993', *Centre national de la cinématographie* 252 (1994), p. 20.

96  Lefevre, 'Une autre vision', p. 66.

## 2   The film

In this chapter, I will examine selected scenes and themes from *La Reine Margot*. Drawing on the contexts of production laid out in the previous chapter, I explore the film's cinematic construction of historical spectacle, Romanticism and aesthetics, gender and sexuality, and myths of the national past. An aesthetically rich text replete with cultural meanings, *La Reine Margot* lends itself to close textual analysis. A careful reading of different aspects of the cinematic text – narrative structure, *mise en scène*, lighting, camerawork, set decoration and locations, sound (music, dialogue and ambient sound), editing, point of view and performance – will tease out how this work of historical fiction generates multiple pleasures and cultural meanings for contemporary audiences. Given that *La Reine Margot* was conceived, produced and sold as a 'super-production', the process of close textual analysis can illuminate the elements contributing to the film's distinctive mode of historical spectacle. In disassembling this compelling spectacle, I delve into how the film constructs power, politics and the past, mythologies of nation, gender, sexuality and the body.

The version of the film used in this analysis is the original 'uncut' French version released on DVD, with the exception of one romantic scene added in for the film's American release. Citations of English dialogue are taken from the English subtitles of the PAL video version. As mentioned in Chapter 1, the plotting, time-frame, political and geographical scope of *La Reine Margot* derives largely from Dumas' novel. With an original running time of two hours and 23 minutes, the film covers a historical period of approximately 20 months. It dramatises the wedding of Marguerite de Valois and Henri de Navarre (18 August 1572), the subsequent massacre of Saint-Barthélemy (particularly the first night of 24 August) and the event's political and personal aftermath for the film's protagonists. The film concludes with the death of King Charles IX and the triumphant return of his successor Henri III (Anjou), and the concurrent execution of La Môle and Coconnas (the actual date of their execution was 30 April 1574, while the king died a month later at the end of May). Before turning to an analysis of specific scenes, I will first present some observations on *La Reine Margot*'s structural organisation.

## The structure of the narrative

As discussed in Chapter 1, Dumas' Romantic dramatisation of the events surrounding the massacre of St-Barthélemy condenses a broad tableau of historical action into personalised relationships and storylines. In contrast with a more 'rational' account of historical event and causality, literary and cinematic historical fiction renders the past legible through intimate relationships. Following Dumas' Romantic aesthetic, these relationships are charged with intensive emotions: passion, hatred, loyalty and betrayal. For Rosenstone, most historical film treats history either as 'document' or as 'drama', both of which tend to frame 'history as the story of individuals'. This strategy constructs for present viewers an identification with the fate of past individuals to demonstrate the 'human' causes and effects of historical problems. Moreover, both documentary and fictional cinematic accounts of the past tend to emotionalise, personalise and dramatise the past.

> Through actors and historical witnesses, it gives us history as triumph, anguish, joy, despair, adventure, suffering and heroism. Both dramatised works and documentaries use the special capabilities of the medium – the close-up of the human face, the quick juxtaposition of disparate images, the power of music and sound effect – to heighten and intensify the feelings of the audience about the events depicted on the screen.[1]

Drawing from Dumas, Thompson's script incorporates three major 'personal' storylines. The first is the monstrous melodrama of the Valois family. The family is headed by the controlling mother figure Catherine de Médicis, whose three wicked sons vie for power while their sister Margot struggles with divided loyalties. Riddled with incest, infighting and infanticide and dominated by an ominous 'foreign' mother, the Valois family could be seen as representing the dissolute and unstable state of the French ruling class of the period.

The second storyline concerns two minor historical figures, the Catholic Coconnas and the Protestant La Môle. Forced to share a bed at the film's outset, the men struggle almost to the death during the massacre; afterward they recover from their wounds under the same roof, forging a bond that holds until death with their joint execution. Bound together by fate, Coconnas' and La Môle's passage from sworn enmity to sworn loyalty transcends political circumstance and religious difference. Significantly, the film begins and ends with these two 'ordinary' characters, whose fates are determined by higher powers. Their reconciliation enacts a symbolic allegiance between the French Catholics and Protestants.

The triangle between Margot, La Môle and Navarre is the film's third 'personal' storyline. The complex ties between these three characters link intimate experience with the broader field of history. A counterpoint to the monstrous Valois men, Perez's La Môle is the film's tragic hero. Handsome and noble, La Môle 'seeks out his own death. He has a magnificent purity amongst all of these monsters.'[2] If the ill-fated La Môle becomes Margot's true love, her beleaguered husband Navarre successfully navigates a precarious position at the Louvre during and after the massacre. A survivor rather than a hero, Navarre does not engage in useless acts of bravery but renounces his faith in order to be spared. He endures insults and threats at court, and bides his time to become, later, one of France's most popular kings: the lore of 'good King Henri' as successor to the Valois dynasty is a piece of popular knowledge that informs present-day French viewers.

At the epicentre of these three storylines is Adjani's Margot. Part of the terrible Valois clan, the Catholic princess takes a dissenting stand to support two Huguenot men, Navarre and La Môle. As the film's central, 'mythic' character, Margot is situated as witness to the events that surround her. Margot is 'transformed' by the horrors of Saint-Barthélemy – especially by finding true love with the Protestant La Môle. Following the mythology discussed in Chapter 1, the film's dramatic focus on a powerful and highly sexual female character privileges a 'boudoir' account of history. The political actions of the actual historical figure are displaced onto a fictional account, where Margot is centrally defined as wife, sister and lover. Physically and emotionally buffeted between the different factions, Margot can be seen as 'an embodiment of France caught between warring factions'.[3]

In order to grasp the narrative organisation of La Reine Margot, it is helpful to consider its structural elements. Narrative cinema is often seen to be made up of a narrative (or story-) line periodically punctuated by sequences of cinematic spectacle. Leger Grindon considers the historical film as a juxtaposition of the personal 'romance' narrative with historical spectacle. If the film's three narrative lines personalise the causal factors and effects of historical events, large-scale spectacle sequences represent broader historical and social forces.

> The spectacle emphasizes the extrapersonal forces (social, economic, geographic, and so forth) bearing on the historical drama. The spectacle's relation to the romance expresses the links between the individual, nature and society, and serves as a vehicle for historical explanation. In contrast to the romance, which is shaped by the plot and characters, the features of the spectacle are period setting – architecture...mass action...and the broad visual landscape.[4]

Chéreau deliberately shot much of the film on an intimate scale close to the faces and bodies of the actors taken up with romance and clandestine trysts. However, cinematic spectacle is also intrinsic to La Reine Margot. Integrated into the film's complex narrative action are three major spectacle sequences: the wedding, the massacre and the hunt. Dramatically, these sequences represent major turning points in the narrative. If the ritualistic, formal wedding as affair of state sets the stage for an explosive proximity between Catholics and Protestants, the subsequent massacre makes manifest the consequences of religious hatred in explosions of kinetic movement and graphic violence.

Later in the film, the hunt interrupts the film's preponderance of gloomy interiors in a daytime woodlands scene. Full of movement and colour, the imagery of the wild boar hunt encapsulates the capricious dynamics of hunting in packs. Initially the dogs relentlessly pursue the boar and corner it, but at the last minute the fortunes of the hunt change and the boar turns on the king – who is deliberately left to his fate by his brothers. It is Navarre who intervenes; throughout the film Navarre is referred to as a 'beast', a 'smelly goat' and even (in the wedding scene) as a 'wild boar'.[5] The hunt could be read as an allegory for Navarre's fortunes where the hunted becomes the hunter. More generally, the hunt vividly manifests the bloodlust lurking near the surface of this society.

In the analysis that follows, I present detailed readings of two of the spectacles that are crucial to the film's status as cinematic event: the wedding and the massacre. Rich in cultural and historical references, these scenes condense some of the film's most compelling qualities as a visceral audiovisual experience. I also offer close readings of several other key sequences, selected partly to correspond to the film's major thematic and stylistic elements: the wedding festivities (femininity and sexuality), La Môle's 'exile' abroad (cultural difference and the international 'scene'), the lovers' clandestine tryst (tragic romance), the feast prior to Anjou's departure (the monstrous family), the poisoning of Charles IX ('homosocial' desire and the suffering male body) and the ending (narrative and symbolic 'closure'). As suggested by the bracketed themes, each section of textual analysis incorporates a discussion of the sequence's cultural and symbolic significances.

### Strange bedfellows: La Môle and Coconnas/Margot's wedding

The film begins with white credits on a black screen, accompanied by a haunting *a capella* arrangement in a minor key for four male voices. A large intertitle announces the year as 1572, and several paragraphs of text follow outlining the political context, setting the stage for the violence to come.

> August 18, a heat wave has fallen over Paris. Thousands of Protestants have come for the wedding. They are invading the inns and the streets. Their dark clothes and looks provoke the Parisians, already on the verge of rebellion. Margot's wedding, a symbol of peace and reconciliation, will be used to set off the greatest massacre in the history of France.

The titles conclude as the music fades out. Voices can be heard off-screen, although the screen remains cloaked in darkness. A flickering torch is waved fleetingly across the black screen, only partially illuminating the face of the bearer, grotesquely contorting it. As he barks out the price of a room, it becomes clear that this is the face of an innkeeper. A series of disorienting medium shots and close-ups are edited rapidly together as the innkeeper and the visitor (Coconnas) ascend a gloomy stairway; in this obscure space we are granted a clear image neither of the men nor of the inn itself.

Grumbling about the influx of Protestants into Paris, the innkeeper shows Coconnas to his room. When the visitor sits on the bed, he surprises another man (La Môle) sleeping, who shouts in surprise and reaches for his sword. In response, Coconnas draws his musket. This scuffle dramatises the brewing tensions in Paris, and anticipates a more violent confrontation that will soon transpire in this room between these men.

In keeping with Dumas' novel, Chéreau's film does not begin with Margot and the royalty but with Coconnas and La Môle, two 'ordinary' characters. In the grimy bedchamber, the men realise not only that they must share a bed but that they belong to opposing religious groups. Descending the stairs with his flickering torch, the innkeeper declares with ill humour: 'There we are. Everyone in the same bed. We're all friends now. Unity is what they want, so set an example!' As the two men settle uneasily to sleep, Coconnas asks La Môle if he has come for the royal wedding, and La Môle replies: 'Margot is an evil whore.' The shared bed of Catholic and Protestant presents a volatile symbolic alliance that parallels that of Margot and Navarre.

From La Môle's insult about Margot (uttered in a shadowy close-up by the man who will be her lover), cut to a close-up of Adjani as Margot in partial profile. She is resplendent in a red gown embroidered in silver, with a stiff white lace ruffle framing a white face mask-like in its composure. In contrast with Margot's heavily powdered alabaster face, her lips are deep red and her blue eyes are downcast; the princess's dark hair is pinned up in an elaborate coiffe decorated with pearls and precious stones. From the spare ambient sound of the inn, a full-voiced chorus with organ accompaniment announces this transition to the wedding scene. In keeping with the characteristic fast-paced, rhythmic editing, the film cuts quickly from close-up to a formally balanced long shot situating Margot centre-frame, kneeling in profile in front of a large group of bishops. Grouped in rows, the religious figures making up this formidable assemblage are clad in ornate gold and red finery and carry sceptres. Most striking in this spectacular tableau are the bishops' tall white mitres, standing out in a bright geometrical pattern against the dark background of the cathedral.

Suspended on the wall behind the priests is a huge crucifix, flanked by two elaborate chandeliers. Presiding over the ceremony in this mighty cathedral, the crucifix sanctifies the tremendous display of the clergy in their finery, marking the great wealth and power of the Catholic Church of the period. (As I will discuss below, the agonies of Christ on the cross prefigures recurring imagery of the suffering male body within a society marked by the pleasures of flesh and power exercised directly on the body in torture and violent death.)

Chéreau does not linger on this 'money shot' of the cathedral setting, costumes and huge cast (complete with its soaring choral accompaniment). After five seconds, cut to a medium shot of the cardinal who is reading the wedding vows. Cut to Auteuil as Navarre in close-up as he assents, then briskly back to the cardinal, who asks the same of Margot. Framed in a profile shot kneeling beside Navarre, Margot (in the foreground) does not respond but holds her head up proudly, her eyes half closed. The silence breaks the brisk rhythm of the ritual, and in the background we see the restless consternation of the king and the other powerful figures seated behind Margot and Navarre. In the scene's first camera movement, a panning shot scans the faces of the film's major players, who turn questioningly to each other: Coligny, Charles IX, Médicis. Finally, a quick swish pan brings the camera to hold on the smug, smiling face of Henri, duc de Guise. Marked out by this jarring camera movement, Guise (as we will learn later) emphatically opposes this union as an arch-Catholic and as one of Margot's lovers.

A marriage of convenience: Margot and Henri de Navarre

As the cardinal repeats the question, the king rises from behind his sister and brusquely shoves her head forwards. Margot's exclamation of surprise is taken for assent and the bishop quickly declares the couple to be man and wife.[6] The music, attenuated during the ceremony, climaxes in a great chorus of 'Hallelujah!' as the wedding party rises. Another striking long shot frames Margot in her elaborate wedding dress walking towards the camera, flanked by bishops, altar boys and other members of the wedding party. The ceremonious choral number continues as the wedding party processes along the aisle towards the great doors of the cathedral. The wedding is attended by a huge crowd: Huguenots, marked out in black, grouped on either side of the the the aisle, and Catholics in their colourful finery of green, red and gold filling the balconies.

In keeping with the scene's rapid editing pace, during the procession there is a constant cutting between ostentatious long shots demonstrating the pomp and pageantry of the occasion and intimate two-shots. This brisk editing breaks the weighty formality and lumbering tempo associated with the spectacle of historical fiction. Chéreau comments that 'there is in fact a very intimate vein in *La Reine Margot*, clandestine relationships, secrets well-guarded by the characters and this interests me more than a large fresco. Actually, what pleased me was the huge contrast between the extremely large and extremely small.'[7]

A fleeting moment of spectacle: the wedding procession

As the wedding party processes along the aisle, a series of exchanges framed in intimate two-shots introduce significant characters and highlight rising tensions. The king declares to Navarre: 'In giving you my sister Margot, I give my heart to all of your faith.' At this point, Anjou inserts his leering face between Charles and Navarre, declaring: 'Welcome to the family, Henri. It's a peculiar one, but not that bad.' Meanwhile, Médicis the queen mother (resembling a spider with her black gown, pale white puffy face and a spiky golden web-like collar) whispers to the lovely young Charlotte de Sauve. Médicis prompts Sauve to invite Navarre to her chambers for his wedding night, referring to her son-in-law as a 'wild boar' and a 'smelly goat'. Confirming these unorthodox sleeping arrangements, Margot admonishes her new husband that this is a 'marriage for peace', and that no one expects her to sleep with him. Meanwhile, the handsome Guise is pictured with his arch-enemy Coligny, and again deep in conversation with the queen mother Médicis.

> *Catherine*: My Catholics and my Protestants, together in God's house. Look, this wedding will fix everything.
> *Guise*: A wedding and a war. That'll fix the French.
> *Catherine*: War? Who talks of war today?
> *Guise:* (Pointing to Coligny) Look at him, Coligny wants war.
> *Catherine:* The king is against war, I know.
> *Guise:* What do you know? The king is Coligny's puppet. Your power is finished. (Cut to Coligny speaking quietly to the king, his arm around the younger man's shoulders.)

Guise and Médicis: an intimate moment of intrigue during the wedding ceremony

With snatches of conversations 'caught' by the camera, this scene's overall effect is of a state ceremony orchestrated for public effect. However, this uneasy pact barely papers over the rifts between hostile factions and personalities. As the great doors of the church open, admitting natural light into this dark scene, the 'Hallelujah' chorus comes to a resounding finale. To conclude the scene on an 'intimate' rather than a 'spectacular' note, Navarre and Margot are framed in close-up and the bride reiterates: 'Don't come to my room tonight!'

These parallel instances of 'strange bedfellows' neatly establish a whole range of stylistic, thematic, narrative and intertextual elements within the first nine minutes of the film. The gloomy lighting, pervasive intrigue and barely dormant violence contribute to a Romantic 'thriller' atmosphere. Following the intertitles a considerable body of narrative and historical exposition is conveyed, and the main characters are systematically introduced. In moving from 'street level' to the Louvre, a structure of parallel storylines is established where Coconnas and La Môle provide a gritty 'preface' to the royal nuptials. In Dréville's 1954 version the duo contribute a humorous, almost slapstick element, and in keeping with 1950s swashbuckling conventions the first scene ends on a dashing fencing match. In contrast, the Romantic atmosphere established in this opening scene of Chéreau's film is much more ominous, with settings and faces all equally obscured in darkness.

The friendship between La Môle and Coconnas forms a structuring element in Dumas' novel and in Dréville's adaptation, but Chéreau's version adds a different inflection. Rather than the humorous disavowal of same-sex desire played out in Dréville's film, in the hands of an openly gay director this ambiguous coupling becomes passionate and intense. Indeed, in his other cinematic works, such as *L'Homme blessé*, *Ceux qui m'aiment prendront le train* or *Son Frère*, Chéreau is fascinated with intensive interactions between men. In *La Reine Margot*, La Môle's and Coconnas' friendship adheres to a dominant masculinist economy within the film. As I will discuss below, I equate this economy with 'homosocial desire', an 'affective or social force' that structures relations among men.[8]

Turning to the wedding scene, it is significant that no face is clearly visible in the film prior to the first close-up of Adjani/Margot at the altar. It is this initial close-up of Margot that diegetically establishes Adjani as the

Renaissance princess. In this initial portrait, Adjani's face is immobile and heavily powdered, producing a mask-like countenance that enacts the mythic fusion of historical figure and actress. This mask-like presentation of the star as an iconic female figure from the past is reminiscent of Garbo's face in the historical film *Queen Christina*;[9] interestingly, the reclusive Adjani is sometimes known as the 'French Garbo'. For Jean-Louis Comolli, the actor fills in the shell of the historical figure, whose body is 'an *empty mask*, and the character will appear later and bit by bit as effects of this mask, effects in the plural, changing, unstable, never quite achieved, thwarted, incomplete'.[10] The mask-like quality of Adjani's face throughout the scene corresponds with Tom Shone's account of Adjani's 'most intriguing beauty':

> Most of her features [are] arranged on a single almond plane, giving her face the implacable countenance of an oriental mask. On screen, Adjani's face is a mask that seems for ever on the point of cracking , and her most memorable roles – in *L'Histoire d'Adèle H, Camille Claudel, L'Été meurtrier* – have divined deep, dark currents of mania, pushing her characters to the brink of collapse.[11]

First glimpsed in her formal wedding attire, Adjani's composed face resembles a mask, and the epic scale of the scene 'places' her at the infamous wedding. Peculiar to historical fiction is an intertextual shadow play between the face and body of the actor and the actual historical figure. As discussed in Chapter 1, Adjani's Margot resonates with many historical, literary, painterly and cinematic 'portraits' (including Moreau's 1954 performance of Margot). Comolli suggests that 'the historical character, filmed, has at least two bodies, that of the imagery and that of the actor who represents him for us. There are at least two bodies in competition, one body too much.'[12] Surrounded by priests within this imposing cathedral, Adjani is introduced into the role of Margot during the film's most elaborate 'period' ceremony. This juxtaposition of historical figure with the actor's face and body also holds for the other characters. Within the first few minutes of the film, the larger than life historical figures of Médicis, Navarre, Charles IX, Guise, Coligny and Anjou are systematically introduced. Auteuil's Henri, like Margot, is deliberately foregrounded in close-up during the wedding ceremony. Soon afterwards, the distinctive panning shot scans the familiar faces of Jean-Hugues Anglade, Miguel Bosè and Pascal Greggory in period costume.

If the ensemble cast are given their entrances during the wedding, it is also the sheer scale of the spectacle that is on display here. Along with the hunt and the wedding party, this is the scene where lavish costumes, music, set decoration and hundreds of extras most directly display the film's exorbitant budget on the screen. With Bregovic's extraordinary score, Bickel's richly textured costumes and hundreds of extras, all the elements of a great period spectacle are in evidence. Yet this scene is oddly unsettling – both in its mockery of the solemn ritual of royal marriage, and stylistically in Chéreau's deliberate refusal to dwell on the characteristic 'money shots' so central to the pleasures of historical fiction as popular entertainment.

The king's violent intervention disturbs the wedding, a normally joyous occasion. The uncooperative bride has been labelled a 'whore' by La Môle even before appearing on-screen. Margot is dressed in riotous red, matching the predominant colour-coding of the marriage in blood red and sombre hues, and contributing to a tangible foreboding. The king's public violence towards his sister within a sacred ritual implies a corrupt and brutal monarchy. A sacred occasion and an affair of state meant to heal religious rifts in the realm, this wedding is symbolically marred from the outset.

The wedding scene closes on Margot's reminder to her new husband that she is not required to sleep with him. Perhaps the bridegroom's disappointment is consonant with many spectators' thwarted expectations for this momentous scene. As with other super-productions, no costs were spared. An interview with the film's production director Jean-Claude Bourlat reveals that no fewer than 800 extras were required to fill the Saint-Quentin basilica (although as a cost-saving measure the lower bodies of seated figures were not costumed in period garb, saving 400 pairs of shoes). Nonetheless, the cost of costumes and set decoration was FF20 million (out of a total budget of FF140 million).[13] Yet, in this scene and throughout the film, Chéreau's rapid-fire editing pattern refuses the generic convention of protracted long shots facilitating appreciation of the sets, costumes and locations. Given the tremendous cost and labour involved in these period production values, this decision seems almost perverse.

Another example of this extravagant expenditure was the preparation of the Bordeaux locations for filming the Paris street scenes. Entire streets of houses were repainted (including agreements with each inhabitant to return the building to its found state), and the roads and the pavements were filled in with dirt.[14] As mentioned above, this director favours the 'intimate' scale of close-ups and two-shots; as a result, the results of elaborate preparation and great cost (both in the wedding scene and in Parisian street scenes shot in Bordeaux) are barely visible.

Interestingly, however, images of period spectacle are crucial to the film's publicity, including spectaculars stills from the wedding: both Margot kneeling in front of the clergy and the wedding party processing towards the camera. Also commonly reproduced in the film's publicity is the close-up of Adjani as Margot in her wedding finery – the mask-like cinematic portrait merging star persona and iconic historical figure. In the next scenes, the immobile mask gives way to a much more animated Margot, who hunts for lovers within her own wedding party and in the streets.

### Wedding festivities and a 'strange' wedding night

After the wedding the gloom of the cathedral gives way to a large and bustling crowd scene, where the wedding celebrations take place outdoors in direct sunlight. Blending with ambient sounds of laughter and chatter, a merry jig can be heard (the source of the music will soon be revealed to be a small musical ensemble). Sombre Protestants rub shoulders with Catholics clad in rich brocades of gold, red and green. Drinking freely, the guests are entertained by all manner of carnival activities: a line of dancers weaves its way through the crowd, while small children play blind man's bluff; later we will see acrobats and wrestling.

To match the change of mood the film language becomes much more fluid, with the camera constantly on the move, adroitly capturing different conversations and dynamics. This chaotic, libidinal scene contrasts with the stiffness and precarious ritual of the previous scene. Here, as in the wedding scene, Chéreau eschews costume film's conventional pleasures of formal dances or spectacular 'money shots' capturing details of period costumes, jewellery and period locations. Rather, Rousselot shoots in close to the faces and bodies of the actors; the camera is jostled among the revellers, creating an atmosphere of claustrophobia, pressing into a dramatic tangle of bodies and faces.

Initially the camera follows Sauve (who in the previous scene was instructed by Médicis to seduce Navarre) as she weaves her way through the crowd. The young woman's progress is accompanied by the sprightly music, which stops abruptly as the camera lights on the imposing figure of Guise; as in the previous scene, Guise is singled out as an ominous figure who will take a central role in the carnage to follow. Next, a reverse shot frames the object of Guise's hungry gaze, Margot and her friend Henriette de Nevers. Like Charlotte they are clad in low-cut party gowns (Margot's in a richly patterned blue and Henriette's in gold), with their hair tumbling loosely around their shoulders in a sensual cascade of black and auburn. This two-shot frames the women's upper torsos and faces, emphasising the tightly laced bodices and ample cleavage – the lacing of Margot's bodice leaves her breasts partly exposed. These dresses are designed for sexual display rather than historical accuracy, as aristocratic women's gowns of the period were characterised by stiff collars and relatively high necklines (along the lines of Margot's high-necked wedding dress). The sunlight illuminates their laughing and self-assured faces, with rouged lips and darting eyes.

Leaning against each other in a playful sexual pose, the two women openly size up the Huguenot men. Consulting a list, they scrutinise the most eligible of Navarre's supporters: Armagnac, Du Bartas, Condé. Laughing, Henriette tells Margot that Du Bartas is only 19 and lives with his sister. Cutting between the women and close-ups of the men who are the objects of their gaze, this scene of predatory looking briefly introduces supporting Protestant characters. Eventually the women's gaze turns to a fearful Navarre across the courtyard, who is flanked protectively by his lieutenants; dressed in black, this cluster of serious men stands out from the colourful, festive crowd. Cut to this group as Coligny tries to persuade Navarre to join him in three days' time in his march against Philip of Spain in the Netherlands. Highly conscious of his precarious position in a hostile court, Navarre keeps his back to the wall and constantly scans the crowd nervously, replying to Coligny: 'Three days? Will I still be alive in three days?'

This conversation is cut short by a jolly reel, and acrobats can be seen in the middle distance over the heads of the crowd. Against this carnival back-drop, several key conversations and confrontation points take place. Sauve invites Navarre to her chambers that night. Meanwhile, Anjou and Guise are pictured wrestling, bare-chested; during a pause in the competition Margot invites Guise to her rooms that night, 'as usual'. Wrestling provides a demonstration of masculine prowess, contributing to a mounting atmosphere of insistent physicality, and a latent violence lurking beneath the party games.

Cut into the raucous, sunlit party scene is a war council in a darkened room, where Coligny attempts to convince the king and his other advisers to go to war against Spain. Returning to the wedding party outside, rising tensions erupt in a stand-off between Navarre and Guise, who is belligerent with Margot's new husband. Navarre, characterised frequently as a 'peasant' and a 'wild boar', uses his greater physical prowess to overwhelm Guise in a violent embrace, holding his opponent's face close as he plants a hostile kiss on his mouth. As the action escalates from the festive atmosphere of laughter and dance to wrestling to aggressive confrontation and talk of war, the men's expressions of mutual hatred underlines the deep rifts among the wedding guests.

As mentioned above, part of the play of historical fiction involves the intercutting of 'romance' and the 'politics' of broader period spectacle, producing a complex composite of historical fact, myth and invention. The tension between the 'personal' and the 'political' can be traced in the editing pattern of this scene, which marks an insistently gendered economy within the film. With their low-cut gowns and lascivious gazes, Margot and Henriette form the focus of a crescendo of sexual energy. In contrast, the sombre Huguenot men taken up with survival strategies on the eve of the massacre. Femininity is associated with seduction, while the male characters are taken up with weighty 'political' concerns. Indeed, within the first third of the

Shooting in close to bodies and faces: Charlotte de Sauve at the wedding party

film the portrayal of Margot adheres to the myth of an amoral and sexually voracious Renaissance princess continually on the hunt for pleasure, and wilfully indifferent to affairs of state (see Chapter 1).

The two-shot of Margot and Henriette at the wedding party is often featured in *La Reine Margot*'s publicity. This is an image of display that is both diegetic (intended for the admirers surrounding the women at the party) and extra-diegetic (addressed to the film's spectator). The two women's gazes are challenging and desiring – even as they offer themselves in an exhibitionist spectacle. This mode of excessive sexual display is reminiscent of the 'come hither' poses in soft-core pornography. Following Dumas, Margot and Henriette are consistently doubled in a pairing that corresponds to the masculine 'couple' of La Môle and Coconnas who will later become the women's lovers. Dominique Blanc's Henriette often presents an amoral 'screen' or 'witness' to Margot's actions. Here, Henriette mirrors and amplifies Margot's sexual display with her explosion of red hair and knowing glances; following pornographic coding, the half-nude women's bodies entwined project an excess of sensuous and inviting feminine flesh. (According to some versions of the Margot legend, Henriette also participated in Margot's many sexual conquests.)[15]

A change in Adjani's Margot can be seen in the wedding party scene. The ritual 'mask' of the wedding scene is offset here by a much 'looser'

Margot and Henriette de Nevers: sexual display and the lascivious female gaze

demeanour that is physical and explicitly sexual. In a performance style reminiscent of earlier roles of highly sexual (and disturbed) women in *L'Été meurtrier*, *Possession* and *Camille Claudel*, Adjani arches her neck and her body, rolling her eyes to exude an ecstatic, almost crazed sexuality. This part of the film resonates with the highly sexual trajectory of the Margot myth that can be traced through pornographic tracts from the 1607 *Le Divorce satyrique* up until recent publications.[16] As Sellier points out, Chéreau's film perpetuates this version of the myth of Marguerite de Valois, deploying some

> rather dubious [references] not found in Dumas' novel… [Chéreau] draws from some of the worst political-pornographic pamphlets under the pretext of a realist vision of the Valois court, making Marguerite a nymphomaniac who goes hunting for men in the streets of Paris when her court lovers fail her.[17]

In this passage, Sellier refers to an incident later during the wedding night. It is worth examining this part of the film in order to explore the treatment of gender and sexuality in *La Reine Margot*. After the wedding party, Margot is borne to her chambers on a litter by the revellers. In a shot from Margot's point of view, we see Guise waiting for her on his knees. Placing Margot above her prospective lovers, the angle of this shot suggests the character's hypnotic power over men. When Margot joins Guise on the floor, the pair is framed in a tight two-shot showing their faces in profile – their two faces almost conjoined as they stroke each others' hair and faces. This particular shot is used throughout the film to indicate the intensive sexual and emotional ties between family members (Médicis and Anjou), friends (the king and Coligny) and sworn enemies (Navarre and Guise's hateful embrace).

In the heat of passion, Margot exclaims: 'Tonight, love me like never before…I want an endless night, I want to see the image of my death amidst my pleasure.' This statement exemplifies the film's recurring theme, which I will return to below, where the intensities of sexual pleasure are linked closely with death. Margot's tryst with Guise is soon interrupted by the arrival of Navarre, who begs his wife to act as his ally. After Navarre's departure, Guise (listening from behind a door) is overcome by jealousy and departs. Margot, still aroused, turns to Henriette exclaiming: 'I need a man tonight!' Laughing wildly, her friend responds: 'We're going out!'

Next, in the scene referenced by Sellier, the two women don masks to prowl the streets of Paris in search of a mate for Margot. A melancholy male solo voice track accompanies a shot of the narrow city streets illuminated with an eerie blue light. It is dusk as the two women recklessly wander the narrow streets in their finery, Margot clad in her embroidered blue gown and carrying a shimmering royal blue cape. The camera follows the women's gazes as they look down at the young Huguenot men; these visitors have nowhere else to go and they line the streets, sitting on the ground. As with the earlier shot of Guise, the camera angle inscribes the women's privilege and power in relation to their quarry. When Margot spies La Môle he returns her gaze, only to be attacked by brigands pursuing his attackers, who have made off with his horse and belongings. After the thieves' escape, Margot picks up his green book that has fallen in the dust and hands it to him as the two square off in an exchange of looks in close-up, with Perez's handsome face becoming fully visible for the first time, even as Margot remains masked. He states: 'They've taken everything,' to which Margot (playing the prostitute) replies: 'It'll be free for you, then.'

The melancholy vocal track fades out with a cut to the pair having intercourse in the alley while Henriette keeps watch. All that can be heard are the loud sounds of their breathing and the distant barking of a dog. La Môle holds Margot roughly against the wall, and a rapid series of shots close in on their bodies and on Margot's masked face, capturing the desperate intensity of this anonymous encounter. Following the prostitute code, Margot refuses to let him kiss her mouth. After orgasm they fall away separately, strangers again, and the camera holds on a close-up of La Môle's face as Margot departs and the music comes up again. As Sellier suggests, this encounter plays on exploitative folklore rather than historical probability, as it is highly unlikely that two young women of the court would wander the streets of Paris unaccompanied (let alone that they would search for sex in the streets).

Within the structure of the film, the debauched wedding night with its intrigue, heightened sexual desires and barely concealed hatred escalates inexorably towards the slaughter that is to follow. Part of the momentum arises from rapid editing and dynamic camerawork that shadows the constant, chaotic movement of bodies and facial expressions. Yet however dynamic the film style, this complex narrative is highly structured through measured repetitions: The initial encounter between La Môle and Coconnas is followed by their later hostile encounter at the inn; also, after the wedding night with Guise and Navarre in the princess's chambers, the wounded La

Môle will later make his way to her boudoir. (Here, the repeated enclosed spaces of inn and boudoir provide an intimate focus within a much broader tableau of intrigue and violence.) Finally, the women's manhunting street scene foreshadows a later sequence, when the women will retrace their steps the morning after the massacre in search of La Môle's body. In their next outing in these narrow streets the women will be masked with white cloths to stifle the stench of death, and these same Protestant wedding guests will line the streets as attractive corpses.

### The spectacle of history: the massacre of Saint-Barthélemy

If *La Reine Margot* injects a new dynamism into historical fiction, it does so in part through a distinctive orchestration of historical event as visceral, violent and immediate *spectacle*. From the opening intertitles viewers are primed for this scene. Throughout the wedding and the subsequent festivities, the film builds inexorably for 40 minutes towards an explosion of violence. The massacre of Saint-Barthélemy overwhelms Chéreau's *La Reine Margot* like a splash of blood in a basin of water. Indeed, Chéreau describes the film's narration through its colour scheme:

> The black, like some living reproach, invades the start of the movie [the wedding and its aftermath], irrigating it like streams spreading through the feasts and through the squares... The black shall disappear little by little, in the great massacre, changing into bloodstained linen – red, once again – then into the milky white of bleak flesh as it is violently roused from sleep; the white of all those corpses piled up in mud, naked, without clothes.[18]

The onset of the massacre is announced by an ominous chiming of the church bells mourning the carnage that (in the present of the viewer) has already happened and yet (in the film's present of 1572) is about to unfold. *Dong...dong...dong...* The scene begins with La Môle peering out of the window of his garret into the deserted streets below at the sound of the bells; his room and the city below are steeped in inky blackness, and only La Môle's gleaming eyes can be seen. The tolling of the bells bridges a cut to Guise, who has been enlisting men (including Coconnas) in the armoury to carry out the king's orders, and he declares: 'It has started.' A loud crash coincides with a cut from Guise to the Protestants' chamber as the soldiers burst in on Navarre and his lieutenants. The soldiers violently shove the

Huguenot leaders into the hallway, and Navarre is singled out and led away. In the confused press of bodies that follows, the Huguenots are visually distinguished from their assassins by their sombre black attire. The soldiers and their victims surge through the palace corridors to the relentless chiming of the bells. Margot appears in medium shot, rushing towards the camera, her face and gown luminously white against the shadowy, torchlit scene of the corridor. A tracking shot follows her in profile as she runs headlong against the flow of the crowd. A series of graphic murders are cut to the rhythmic atonal chanting of a male chorus: Du Bartas is dispatched on the steps with a sharp sword thrust through the torso; Nançay, captain of the guard, holds a woman from behind and slashes open her throat with a flourish; with a great guttural cry, a line of the king's soldiers charges, skewering a terrified group of Huguenots with their lances. On the soundtrack, we hear the clash of metal against metal, stone and flesh and a confusion of guttural cries.

Bregovic's powerful score contributes centrally to the intensity of the film as a whole, and nowhere is the music more forceful than during the massacre scene. Especially composed for this scene, Bregovic's 'La Nuit de Saint-Barthélemy' combines rhythmic medieval sonic signifiers (the apocalyptic chiming of the bells, an *a capella* chanting of a male chorus) with haunting minor melodies and harmonies. These vocals were based on Corsican chants, and as the scene progresses synthesisers gradually build aural volume around the spare and rhythmic medieval sounds. Later, when the soldiers rush through the narrow streets of Paris, drum rolls add a military dimension to the score, punctuated by diegetic gunshots.

Throughout this graphic and precisely edited sequence of 18 minutes' duration, the relentless thrust of daggers, lances and swords is captured, in close to the body, in medium shots. Rapid editing splices in close-ups of the victims' faces as they perish – young, beautiful, incredulous that life has ended so suddenly. For example, the camera captures Du Bartas at his moment of death, recalling the young man's introduction by name during the wedding festivities. Meanwhile, the camera holds on the handsome face of another young Protestant as he dies; another shot briefly captures an array of pale faces framed in dark collars as they fall in a heap, felled by the soldiers' lances.

These faces captured at the moment of death *personalise* and *intensify* violent acts of history, in the process renewing them and making them *of the present.* In an interview, Chéreau's states: 'If I make films, it is in order to photograph faces.' In contrast with the conventional elaborate theatrical sets of historical fiction that place the audience at an emotional distance from the characters and events depicted, the director 'wanted to be immediately with the characters, at the heart of their tension, of their own time'.[19] Drawing upon a theatrical tradition and foregrounding an ensemble of accomplished actors, an expressive filming of the actors' faces constructs an intensive proximity to the subjective experience of the past.

Historical fiction and literary adaptation proceed in the 'future perfect' – that is, most of the audience is already familiar with the events depicted. The pleasure in the viewing resides not in narrative suspense but in the freshness and *style* of the tale's telling. Films such as *La Reine Margot* or *Cyrano de Bergerac* present familiar tales and histories reinvented as dynamic cinematic spectacle. Lionel Trilling notes that cultural texts representing past times and ways of life are 'in some sense *dead*, and it is in their being so that we find their significance. This significance consists in the paradox that their motion is to be seen as fixity; its evanescence has, through representation, become permanence.'[20] Indeed, part of the challenge of 'filmed history' involves injecting immediacy into times already dead and gone, in reinventing past events as somehow 'live'. We could think of this as reinserting historical event and experience into the contemporary flow of time – the historical period and sensibility of the filmmaking, and most importantly, perhaps, into the duration and sensation of watching.

A return to the 'Marianne' imagery: Margot as horrified witness to the massacre

With its distinctive vision of 'sound and fury' as exemplified by the massacre scene, Chéreau's *La Reine Margot* is deliberately set apart from the 1950s 'tradition of quality' (and, indeed, from the more recent pastoral and nostalgic literary adaptations such as *Jean de Florette* and *L'Amant*). Dréville's *La Reine Margot* relied on long shots and medium shots to display the genre's elaborate sets, costumes and spectacular set pieces; close-ups were rare, even for the film's stars. The film's luminous studio lighting was designed to set off elaborate costumes, sets and large-scale scenes. Finally, Dréville handled the massacre at a formal and emotional remove, in long shots with extended duel sequences in the Louvre; scenes on the streets of Paris showed bonfires and naked women being thrown alive into the Seine.

In contrast, Chéreau produces a disturbing visceral proximity that is at once dynamic, carefully orchestrated and intensely beautiful. With its gritty and mobile 'naturalism' comparable to Rappeneau's *Cyrano de Bergerac*, Chéreau's film invokes Romantic historical genre painting. Accordingly, the Louvre in this production is full of dark corners, barely illuminated by flickering torchlight, while the streets of Paris become labyrinthine corridors of death. The action is plunged in shadow, particularly during the night of Saint-Barthélemy, even as the characters' motivations and the precise historical causes of the violence are cloaked in obscurity.

Chéreau's reference to Romantic paintings in his *mise en scène*, lighting and composition builds upon the cultural memories embedded in these iconic French works. As signifiers of the national past, Peter Brooks argues that paintings such as *Liberty Leading the People* by Delacroix resonate

A painterly spectacle of death: allegorical images of 'genocide'

within a famous narrative trajectory (the revolution of 1830), while crystallising a dramatic historical moment. This 'moment', for Brooks, represents a synecdoche imprinted in the memory of the nation: '[T]he moment which perfectly illustrates a narrative significance – and more: which concentrates and condenses in itself, in a way that narrative sequences cannot, the essence of an event, the plastic figuration of its profound meaning.'[21]

The massacre sequence of La Reine Margot projects the heightened intensity of the painterly historical moment harnessed into the cinematic flow of time. Cinematographer Rousselot evokes Delacroix's scenic sense, transposing the implied motion of the painter's compositions into dynamic cinematic motion through mise en scène, montage and rapid-fire editing. The constant movement of bodies and camera, the intercutting between locations and vantage points on the action, are animated and punctuated by music and diegetic sound. Here, Chéreau deploys a jumble of disparate visual and aural signifiers – vivid Romantic imagery, the 'Eastern' sonic signifiers of Bregovic's music, the 'religious and sensuous' imaginary of Elizabethan drama showing 'death alongside the pleasures of the flesh'.

Yet, in this postmodern rendering of the past as a 'pastiche' of different historical and cultural references, La Reine Margot as vertiginous cinematic spectacle generates a deliberate confusion about the place and time of the violence (and its causes and meanings). In this respect, Saint-Barthélemy as cinematic spectacle generates a sensory immediacy of past violence for the contemporary spectator. Anchored in the dominant discourse of historical 'progress', the contemporary viewer looks back in horror at the 'barbarity' of the 16th century. Yet the film's insistence on the proximity of the violence and its evocation of 20th-century 'tableaux of death' raise issues of historical context and accountability.

David Riches interprets cultural meanings of violence through visual and physical dynamics, notably the relationship between performer, victim and witness.[22] Within any historical or cultural context, 'performers' of violence will justify their actions: at the time of Saint-Barthélemy, the perpetrators cited decrees by the Catholic Church and (more ambiguously) the king. Yet ultimately, for Riches, the victims and (dissenting) witnesses within any society demarcate acts as 'violent' or 'illegitimate'. Cinematic meanings are centrally constructed through patterns of looking, and La Reine Margot situates the complicitous and voyeuristic gaze as integral to the tableaux of violence. Embedded within the massacre scene is a complex encoding of point of view that aligns the spectator ambiguously with both 'dissenting' and 'participating' perspectives on the violence.

With the dirty work carried out by soldiers such as Nançay and Coconnas, the powerful (and culpable) figures of Anjou and Guise are pictured in the thick of the atrocities without dirtying their hands. Anjou grins odiously, showing a sadistic pleasure in the horrors that he has helped to orchestrate. Meanwhile, Margot's friend Henriette is pictured (improbably) wandering the streets in the company of Coconnas and a cohort of soldiers. Surveying Coconnas' actions with a lascivious and admiring gaze, she goads him on in his frenzy of bloodshed. At one point, when a hapless Huguenot is violently dispatched, a cut to a reaction shot shows Henriette laughing, her ample, exposed white bosom heaving in excitement. Afterwards, she declares to Margot: 'Danger is like rage, it turns me on!'

Henriette's response suggests how spectators of violent acts – and images? – may revel in the spectacle. In so doing they help to perpetuate the violence even though their hands remain clean. Particularly troubling is the vilification of the female character who finds pleasure in the violence without taking part, a dynamic (concurring) with a vein of misogyny running throughout the film (more on this below). In contrast, Margot functions as a sympathetic witness to the horrors of religious intolerance. With her white dress and luminous face, Margot stands out in the dark confusion of the massacre as a 'Marianne' symbol. This scene recalls the painting *Liberty Leading the People*, where the shining figure of Marianne

Dutch Protestants in Rembrandt's idealised light

stands above the carnage holding the flag of France. This framing of Adjani recalls the long-standing tradition of a beautiful and heroic young woman 'embodying' the nation – and, indeed, of film stars pictured as Marianne. This iconography informs the 1994 film, but the painting's heroic imagery is confounded. Margot is buffeted by cruel, bloodthirsty forces beyond her control, her gown progressively soaking up the blood of the carnage around her.

Interestingly, the other figure consistently framed as a witness is Navarre's little page, Orthon. I would argue that this boy's gaze, more than that of Margot, represents the film's ethical vision. As he accompanies Navarre, Margot and La Môle, Orthon is almost entirely silent, his face angelically lit by the illuminated cubes he carries. Unlike the actual historical figures, the minor character of Orthon is not implicated in the political fortunes of the times. Protected by his youth (and his connection with Navarre), the Huguenot page is the only character to move easily between the different camps, always watching, almost always silent. As with the young boy invented by Rappeneau in his 1989 adaptation of *Cyrano de Bergerac*, the male child could be seen to represent the future, and it is his vision of these iconic events that provides the viewer with the 'purest' perspective on the action.

After the massacre, Orthon accompanies Margot and Henriette as they retrace their steps from the previous night in search of La Môle's body among the corpses. An elegaic choral number with female voices comes up on the soundtrack, while the blue early morning light beautifully illuminates the bodies lining the narrow streets. From the surging and rhythmic editing and music of the massacre, the camerawork here becomes more fluid, suggesting the gazes of characters searching for loved ones. As we move through the streets with Margot, Henriette and Orthon, we see the faces and bodies of the dead. Displayed in a painterly spectacle of death, all the corpses are young and beautiful. Moreover, from the all-male cohort in the streets the night before, many women's bodies now number among the dead.

After these elegaic street scenes, the bodies are transported in carts to mass graves. As with the piles of corpses in *Le Colonel Chabert* (set during the French–Russian Napoleonic wars in 1807), the camera lingers on the streets of Paris and the wide corridors of the Louvre littered with corpses.

Anchored in a dark moments of French history, these films evoke troubled, violent 'sites of memory'. Returning to infamous past events embedded in classic literature (*Le Colonel Chabert* was written by Honoré de Balzac), these films contribute to the ongoing production of mythologies of the national past. Yet the bleak vision of *La Reine Margot* also gestures beyond the parameters of the nation.

This field of mass graves piled with naked corpses evokes both Holocaust imagery and more recent mass murders in Bosnia. When the bodies are stripped of their period garb, these images invoke an elegaic, timeless vision of mass death. In this way, *La Reine Margot* presents an allegorical vantage point on past and present intolerance. In the wake of the 1980s and 1990s rise of the National Front in France, Chéreau's film sides with the victims of the 'oppressed' minority. This position is supported by the intertextual persona of Adjani; with her dramatic insistence on her Algerian roots, the star is a well-known critic of French racist and xenophobic tendencies. Further, Chéreau insists on the parallels between 16th-century and contemporary contexts:

> a refined and heinous period that is also our period – that, is today – where wars of religions still exist, where one nation can split into irreversibly hostile and murderous Catholics and Protestants, where two neighbouring nations can massacre one another in the very heart of Europe.[23]

For Riches, acts deemed 'violent' mark symbolic disorder and illegitimate behaviour, where violence itself is 'efficacious in action [as a political means] and potent in imagery'.[24] This theorist notes the specificity of violence as a *visible* marker of power through the 'tell-tale marks of physical distress it leaves'.[25] Part of the affective force of Chéreau's cinematic depiction of the massacre stems from these visible signs of illegitimate power applied directly onto the body. If violence signals disorder in the French national past or the European present, the visible effects of the disequilibrium are played out through dynamics of suffering, bleeding and exalted bodies.

### The international scene: exile and difference

This section addresses the film's cinematic treatment of religious, cultural and gender differences, with specific reference to La Môle's sojourn in

Amsterdam and the characterisation of Médicis, the foreign queen mother. After recovering from wounds sustained during the massacre, La Môle sets out on a journey that most directly encapsulates the international political context within the film. After the horrors of the massacre and the cloying intrigue at the Louvre, his journey offers a moment of daylit respite in pleasing seascapes and landscapes. La Môle is initially pictured landing by rowing boat on an unnamed coast (probably the white cliffs of southern England); then he travels to Amsterdam to meet Dutch Protestant allies and survivors of the massacre. In the Netherlands, the hero is pictured on a dappled grey horse galloping across a flat plain with a windmill in the distance. The muted colours and composition the shot resemble 17th-century Dutch landscape paintings, such as the work of Jacob van Ruisdael.

Cut to an interior scene, where La Môle meets with a group of Protestants: men, women and children all dressed in the sombre garb of their faith. La Môle is welcomed by Condé and Armagnac, who have survived the massacre, and Condé explains how the Dutch Protestants have been forced to practise their religion in seclusion due to Spanish repression. In the face of Condé's pessimism, La Môle passionately advocates resistance. He insists that Huguenots from all over France would join their cause if they could free Navarre from his house arrest at the Louvre. Surprisingly, it is Mendès, an exiled Spanish Jew, who offers the required financial support for the expedition. Mendès recounts that, although his family converted to Catholicism years ago, his marriage with a Catholic woman is still illegal within the arch-Catholic Spain. He concludes: 'They want the blood to remain pure. I could imagine giving you the money to rescue Navarre, even if I don't share his religion.'

Appearing neither in Dumas' novel nor in historical accounts of the period, Mendès is Chéreau's invention. Given the similarities between the massacre scene and Holocaust imagery, the interpolated Jewish character underlines a parallel between the 16th-century religious persecution of the Huguenots and the Holocaust. This parallel derives from a similar analogy in Heinrich Mann's *The Novel of Henri IV*, a reference frequently cited by Thompson and Chéreau.

In the Amsterdam scene, the Protestants are shown to possess an idealised humility and dignity arising from great suffering. The mild-mannered Mendès is clad in the black garb of the Protestants, his face framed by a white ruffle and illuminated with natural light against an obscure background. Chéreau notes Rembrandt's influence for the Protestant figures, and nowhere is this inflection more marked than in the faces and lighting in this scene. The wood-panelled room is lit with warm beams of natural light from the windows – a quality of light recalling interior scenes painted by Dutch artists such as Vermeer. Peaceful clusters of children, women and men reading, praying and listening gravely to the political fortunes of the Protestants across Europe invoke ordinary people of all ages and nationalities caught up in the repression of the Counter-Reformation.

The lighting, costumes and composition of the Amsterdam encounter contrast sharply with the Louvre's murky shadows and excesses of violence and perverse sexuality. Médicis' Valois brood is doomed to die out childless, whereas the Protestants are depicted throughout the film as 'believers' who will survive and prosper regardless of persecution. Significantly, the only other depiction of families, children and community is found when Navarre returns to his kingdom to convert back to his Protestant faith. From the ostentatious wedding onwards the Catholic Church is consistently associated with wealth and corruption; in contrast, Navarre's conversion takes place in the idealised pastoral setting of a country church.

It is possible to read this natural light on the Protestant faces – Rembrandt's light illuminating the face of the individual against an obscure background – as an idealised light[26] of rationality contrasting with the film's predominant obscurity and barbarism. As mentioned above, we find this light earlier in the film. On his wedding night, Navarre makes his way to Margot (because 'God told him to talk with her'), and his way is lit by Orthon and two other Protestant pages. The boys hold semi-opaque boxes open at the top containing candles, and the light shines up, reverentially illuminating the faces of the light-bearers and Navarre. Rather than idealising Protestantism per se, this light could be seen as representing religious tolerance (or perhaps the secular principles of post-revolutionary France). Significantly, this light is associated with the future Henri IV, who will be the architect of the Edict of Nantes.

From the Amsterdam episode, there is a transition to a starkly contrasting scene. The queen's odious perfumer and poisoner, René, carefully examines the entrails of a slaughtered animal to tell the future; his hands and arms are soaked in blood. A dark figure in the foreground, Médicis lurks anxiously as he predicts 'three deaths [of Médicis' sons] followed by decay. Henri de Navarre will rule in their place.' Shrouded in darkness, the spider-like Médicis fades into the shadows with her widow's robes. Her hair, receding far back on her skull, leaves bare a death-like mask of a face with heavy-lidded eyes full of cunning and malevolence. Known in her youth as a great beauty, the Italian leading actress Virna Lisi is convincingly transformed in this film into an 'incarnation of Catherine de Médicis, ugly, old and venomous'.[27] Whereas the film's other non-French characters (the Dutch Protestants and the Spanish Jew) are depicted with compassion and respect, the film's account of this influential Italian is laced with misogyny and xenophobia. In contrast with the idealised framing of the Dutch Protestants, Médicis, with her superstitions and poisons, seems a throwback to the dark brutality and violence of medieval times.

Although historians have described Médicis as a moderating influence during the Wars of Religion (see Chapter 1), in Dumas' novel (as in Dréville's and Chéreau's films) she is at the centre of all plots and poisonings: Médicis plays a central role in instigating the massacre, sends the assassin Maurevel to assassinate Coligny and instigates two attempts on Navarre's life through poison. In Dréville's film, Françoise Rosay's black-clad Médicis portrays a formidable and vicious force. For Sellier, Chéreau's characterisation of Médicis presents 'a perfect image of death that brings us to a powerful link in our culture between the mother and death: the mother, in giving life, also gives death'; Lisi's 'death mask' projects an image where 'the powerful woman is literally death'.[28]

Médicis' vendetta against Navarre ultimately leads to the accidental poisoning of her son; infanticide (in this case also regicide) is the ultimate consequence of a woman crazed with power. Significantly, Médicis' counterpoint in the film is Charles' loyal Huguenot nurse. Even after the other

Stolen pleasures: Margot and La Môle in a rare romantic tryst (this image was used later to promote the film in the US)

Huguenots have fled the Louvre, Charles' nurse remains at the king's bedside, even after he banishes the guilty Médicis.

La Reine Margot is marked by an extreme ambivalence around female agency and sexuality, and the articulation between femininity and death is not limited to the figure of Médicis. Chéreau's film corresponds with a long-standing aesthetic and symbolic articulation of femininity and death. Elisabeth Bronfen posits that, in Western culture,

> the feminine body is culturally constructed as the superlative site of alterity [and] culture uses art to dream the deaths of beautiful women. Over representations of the dead feminine body, culture can repress and articulate its unconscious knowledge of death which it fails to foreclose even as it cannot express it directly.[29]

This fascination with the death of a beautiful woman recurs in Sauve's terrible death by poison later in the film. Whereas in Dumas' novel, the poisoner changes his mind and replaces the poisoned rouge at the last minute, in Chéreau's film the young woman dies a horrible death, foaming at the mouth and writhing in agony.

Bronfen's psychoanalytic reading identifies a repressed cultural fear of death arising in this recurring aesthetic trope; death, projected onto the body of the female 'other', is both simultaneously examined and disavowed. As with the sudden appearance of female corpses in the streets of Paris after the massacre, the filmmaker's gratuitous inclusion of a young woman's horrible death accentuates the film's aesthetic and symbolic articulation between femininity and death. Within a film suffused with death and suffering, Bronfen's analysis is suggestive in its attention to the gendering of death – and its account of the unconscious processes propelling a cultural fascination with death. I will return to the film's specific articulation of death, desire and sexuality below.

## Clandestine romance: La Môle and Margot

If powerful femininity is a site of great ambivalence and is frequently associated with death in La Reine Margot, Margot herself is an interesting exception. In contrast to the other major female roles (Médicis as murderous mother; Sauve as Navarre's mistress who dies a gruesome death; Henriette as lascivious witness to violence), Margot's character is afforded some complexity. As witness to the horrors of Saint-Barthélemy and especially in finding 'true love' with La Môle, she is transformed from wanton seductress to a righteous woman who sides with the oppressed Huguenots. The idea of a 'transformation of the self' through love is a key romantic convention.[30] Dumas' star-crossed lovers belong to another compelling romantic trope where 'unfulfilled passion and unhappy love exercise a stronger effect on the cultural imagination, [leaving] an impression of greater intensity' than happy resolutions.[31]

Yet, in *La Reine Margot*, a film brimming with sensuality and passion, heterosexual romance is given short shrift. In a film running for well over two hours, the encounters between Margot and La Môle are limited to four short trysts: their initial encounter in the street, La Môle's sanctuary in Margot's chambers during the massacre, a brief meeting in Paris after La Môle's return from Amsterdam and finally, the lovers' final secret meeting at the country manor. The latter, the most developed sequence, is the focus of this analysis. As I will elaborate in the next chapter, the insignificance of Margot and La Môle's romance was seen by the American distributors as a major weakness. As a result, the film was re-edited to increase the romantic content for American release. In the process, the lovers' final meeting (described here) was extended. Moreover, an image not included in the original French version – the lovers wrapped in a red cloth – was used as the key marketing image for American publicity.

Like La Môle's expedition to Amsterdam, this lover's tryst marks a quiet interlude within an overwhelmingly claustrophobic and violent film. This secluded encounter exemplifies what Lynne Pearce calls the 'romantic love chronotope', a narrative convention of space/time that 'exists apart from the "historical" lives of the characters, but into which they all are liable to be swept as into a black hole. This chronotope of romantic love … [occurs in what Bakhtin calls] "empty time": a spatio-temporal corridor running "outside" or "beyond" the diachronic processes of the material world.'[32] The separateness of the romantic tryst is established in a long shot of Margot awaiting her lover, alone in a huge, empty room lit only by three candles. Underlining the lonely heroine's anticipation, a plaintive solo female vocal is heard on the soundtrack; soon, the arrival of La Môle and Coconnas is announced by the pounding of horses' hooves outside. Cut to an external shot, where a dark rider gallops up a hill to a country manor that is silhouetted against the evening sky.

The action shifts inside, where Margot embraces her lover, weeping with joy. In a tight close-up, Margot's white blouse and pale face and La Môle's darker face stand out against the gloomy background of the room. Margot believes that she has escaped the Louvre to join her lover for good, but the joy of this reunion is marred when La Môle informs her that she must return to the Louvre (due to Navarre's thwarted escape). This news means the imminent separation of Margot and La Môle, as well as their companions Henriette and Coconnas, who will never see each other again. At this point, a cut to a medium shot reveals Margot's companion Henriette sitting discreetly by a window; she lifts her head upon hearing of their return to Paris, and an exterior shot shows her lover Coconnas departing at a gallop into the night.

Here, the action returns briefly to Paris, where Charles invites Navarre to meet his mistress and infant son. Charles' secret life and the lovers' quiet interlude mark stolen moments of possibility for these royal figures – moments especially poignant for their impending rupture through premature death. In a temporal ellipsis to the next morning, we return to La Môle and Margot naked on a mattress on the floor of the manor. This long shot is illuminated by the morning light streaming in through the window; Margot sits upright behind her lover, holding him. Draped on the mattress is a blood-red cloth that stands out against the muted colours of the scene, and Margot's skin gleams porcelain white against La Môle's lean, darker body. The quiet, haunting female vocal (a reprise from the evening before) is the only sound except for the lovers' breathing and their discussion of the future: If their plot succeeds Margot will be queen of Navarre.

*Margot:* You'll be my master and my subject.
*La Môle:* I love you as you are now. Naked, in exile, forgotten by all. No past, no future…no family, no fancy clothes to bury love.
*Margot:* I'm on your side, with the victims. I won't go back to the killers. (Accenting this point, a haunting chorus joins the single voice on the soundtrack.)
*La Môle:* I'll never be your subject.

La Môle takes Margot in his arms; their lovemaking is filmed in tight shots of their entwined bodies, beautifully lit by natural light. La Môle is on top with Margot in a more traditional (and submissive) position than seen in her earlier sexual exploits. Margot's body is largely covered by that of La Môle, who rises mid-coitus to stand briefly in a full-frontal nude pose, then crouches in the middle of the room. The camera lingers on his crouching body, framed by an empty picture frame leaning against the stone wall. Within this conventional love scene, the sparseness of the set and La Môle's theatrical poses signal an avant-garde theatre aesthetic.

As with the scene where the injured La Môle arrives in Margot's chambers, it is his body, writhing in pain or in pleasure, that is the object of erotic contemplation. In keeping with the film's overriding fascination with the naked male body, Margot is left prostrate on the bed as the camera follows the well-hung Perez. Tellingly, in Chéreau's original version, this brief scene ends with the nude crouching shot of La Môle (with Margot no longer in the frame). The truncated nature of this love scene, including the sidelining of the female figure aligns with the film's 'homosocial' economy.

For the film's American release, however, this scene is extended outside the manor, with the nude lovers draped in a blood-red cape. The pair is first framed outside the hilltop manor, looking out over a lovely green valley in the early morning light. A cut to a frontal medium shot frames the lovers' faces and torsos. In this signature image used on the American film poster, Perez' brown torso and Adjani's gleaming white shoulders stand out against the blood-red cloth. In their nakedness and calm, the lovers share a transcendent quality of innocence and purity possible only in this otherworldly 'chronotope of romantic love'.

As discussed in Chapter 1, Adjani's star image exemplifies the 'luminosity' of white female film stars. In his discussion of 'whiteness', Dyer also addresses how cinematic lighting often constructs a relationship where a darker male romantic lead is 'illuminated by the white woman'.[33] In *La Reine Margot*, it is in fact La Môle who is consistently conferred a 'purity' of spirit and intent within a monstrous milieu, but Margot's radiance at this particular moment in the film marks her 'redemption' through true love. After a night with her lover, Margot is transformed from a sex-crazed 'whore' into a tranquil (and passive) member of an idealised cinematic heterosexual couple.

In a series of intimate close-ups, the scene closes with a romantic exchange. Commenting on rumours that 'death always takes [Margot's] lovers', La Môle asks of Margot: 'Promise you won't forget me, the one you shouldn't have loved.' This moment touches on the *pathos* and symbolic resonance of lovers from different camps – a trope exemplified by Romeo and Juliet and in costume film by Visconti's classic *Senso* (1953). Yet this rather bland scene, added on retrospectively, lacks conviction. Its clichéd romantic imagery and dialogue jars with *La Reine Margot*'s resolutely unsentimental affective landscape. Although the film includes a full roster of Romantic iconography (the dashing rider arriving on horseback to meet his lover, the deserted country house as secluded site of encounter, beautiful countryside, the anguish of star-crossed lovers in their final meeting) the pleasure and emotional resonance associated with these elements is systematically confounded.

As with the wedding sequence, Chéreau maintains a rapid pace of editing that refuses to linger on period settings, costumes and landscapes. The country manor is stripped as bare as an empty stage, we barely glimpse the lush countryside, and the final lovers' tryst is curiously lacking in passion – even in its later more 'romantic' version. In contrast, Rappeneau's super-productions *Cyrano de Bergerac* and *Le Hussard sur le toit* place tragic romance at the heart of their epic tales. In stark contrast with *La Reine Margot*, *Le Hussard sur le toit* offers extensive footage of the stunning landscapes of Provence; here, scenic elements of landscape, period towns and empty country manors are absolutely pivotal to the film's romantic narrative. While Chéreau's film retains an auteurist refusal of the popular pleasures of the period epic, Rappeneau's film embraces them.

The homosocial economy: Coconnas' and La Môle's passionate bond

### The monstrous family

The monstrous Valois clan is central to Dumas' and, in turn, Chéreau's 'intimate' plotting of the past. Nowhere are the grotesque family dynamics better displayed than in the feast celebrating Anjou's departure for Poland. Here, all pretences of civility have been abandoned after the king's betrayal by his two brothers at the hunt. In reprise of the earlier wedding party, we are ushered musically into the feast with a lively flute theme performed by a small ensemble dressed in red. The guests mingle in their finery, nibbling on an elaborate array of food and drink. As with the wedding feast, the camera follows a young woman into the room through the press of bodies. As she passes into a corridor, the camera holds on a tight two-shot of Médicis and Anjou, who are sequestered away in a dark antechamber.

Mother and son are locked in a strange embrace, Médicis holding her favourite son's face while he weeps. Stroking his chest excitedly and kissing him repeatedly around the mouth, Médicis murmurs how much she will miss him. Held for several seconds, this exchange is imbued with the intensity of two lovers about to be parted. Their intimacy is interrupted as Charles proposes a toast to all the 'kings' in the family: after their treachery at the hunt, Charles is sending his brothers away. The camera cuts rapidly between the faces of Alençon, Anjou and Guise to register their tense responses.

The violence of Anjou who was closely associated with the arch-Catholic faction that engineered the massacre, comes closer to the surface on the eve of his banishment. A flowing white shirt open to reveal his muscled torso, Anjou's greasy hair hangs around his face; he wears a heavy cross and women's earrings. Menacingly circling Navarre, Anjou taunts the smaller man for being a cuckold while Margot carries on an affair with La Môle. The other guests form a watchful circle around them and the camera follows the restless pacing of the actors in rising conflict. When Margot intervenes in Navarre's defence, Anjou shoves her into the arms of Guise and Charles, who hold her fast. Anjou slaps his sister hard across the face and she is thrown bodily between Alençon, Anjou and Guise. Her clothes torn, Margot is pushed to the floor. She screams for Charles to intervene, but he simply observes, detached but not innocent.

In this violent semblance of a gang rape, the incestuous relations between sister and brothers are revealed as each claims to have left his mark on her body during their sexual exploits as children. Margot struggles wildly and Alençon and Guise pinion her arms; Anjou brusquely pulls up her dress, exposing the lower part of her body to reveal Charles' 'mark' high up on her thigh. Margot screams at Anjou: 'You're just a dog wearing women's jewellery!' During this violation the camera stays close to the actors' faces and bodies, registering unveiled sadism, hatred and lust within this terrible family. The abuse comes to a halt only when Charles suddenly collapses on the floor, writhing in agony.

Insofar as the monarchy embodies the security, morality and longevity of the nation, the Valois family paint a dark picture of France during a troubled historical period. The fatherless family headed up by an odious foreign mother suggests a state lacking legitimate, mature male leadership. Chéreau's cinematic metaphor of a fatherless family controlled by a perverse and ruthless mother resembles Visconti's *The Damned*, where a German industrialist family embodies the decadence, ruthlessness and perversity of Germany during the rise of Hitler.

As in *The Damned*, the cinematic parallel between family and state in *La Reine Margot* extends into perversion. The sexual mythology of the Valois family has historically included allegations of Margot's incestuous liaisons with her brothers,[34] and of Anjou's sexual preference for boys.[35] Although Dumas' novel avoids the taint of incest and homosexuality, in Dréville's 1954 film Daniel Ceccaldi's Anjou is a 'sissy' villain. In turn, Chéreau's film incorporates much more of this sordid sexual mythology. This shameful episode prior to Anjou's departure is overseen by a cold and perverse 'foreign' mother who desires her favourite son while turning a blind eye to her sons' abuse of their sister. Throughout this attack Médicis lurks in the shadows, only intervening weakly to say: 'Not in public!'

Meanwhile, the doomed Valois brothers present a bizarre assortment of evil and perversion brought to life by bravura performances, especially by Anglade and Greggory. As Anjou, Pascal Greggory depicts a dangerous bully whose arrogant, strutting masculinity is rendered suspect by his woman's earring. With his greenish, sickly face, Julien Rassam's Alençon is meek and silent, but ultimately no less malevolent. Finally, the weak and capricious Charles is alternately childlike, charming, vicious and grossly irresponsible. Even as he sets in motion and then denies responsibility for the massacre, Charles tolerates humiliation. Although he is particularly fond of his sister, the eldest brother is also implicated in the allegations of incest.

If Médicis emerges as a monstrous mother and her sons exude spoilt malevolence, what is Margot's role in this scene? It could be argued that this scenario provides background to her characterisation as a young woman whose voracious sexual appetites arise from a childhood of sexual abuse. As mentioned above, within this psychological trajectory, Margot is transformed by true love from an indiscriminate seductress to a 'good woman'. Indeed, she cries out during her brothers' attack that only La Môle has taught her about love and pleasure.

Yet there is something more sinister afoot in this disturbing scene. Publicly re-enacting alleged incestuous relations within the Valois family for the titillation of the court, this mock 'gang rape' ultimately plays to the audience – just as Margot and Henriette's display in the wedding scene was ultimately oriented towards the cinema audience. For Sellier, this scene suggests less a denunciation of male violence than 'a certain complicity with the pleasure of these men who join forces to humiliate a woman'.[36] In particular, it is worth noting that, during this ritual humiliation, the point of view is not Margot's but alternates between the vantage points of the attackers and the audience. As camera angle and point of view help to construct patterns of identification, the audience is positioned as a voyeur – or, worse, an attacker.

Adjani's Margot is placed at the epicentre of *La Reine Margot* through the intermingling of star persona and mythology. She is also the central eponymous character, who is attributed an ambiguous power through her assertive female sexuality and privileged gaze, which is highlighted early in the film. Yet, alongside the figure of Médicis discussed above, this fascinating and compelling image of powerful femininity is also a site of tremendous ambivalence. I would argue that this scene enacts a kind of ritual humiliation and debasement of both the character and the star herself. The over-presence of Adjani-as-star and the titillating mythology of 'Margot' preclude the development of Marguerite de Valois as a complex character or a historical player. And ultimately, Adjani's Margot is displaced by a masculinist economy of power, corporeality and aesthetics that is the subject of the final section of this chapter.

## The suffering male body: La Môle and Charles IX

I conclude this chapter with an analysis of two strikingly similar scenes: the agony of La Môle in Margot's chambers during the massacre, and Charles on his deathbed. Both scenes foreground the suffering male body through expressive imagery that powerfully juxtaposes death and desire. Connected with the intensive bonds between male characters, this imagery condenses the film's overarching 'homosocial' economy. To begin with La Môle, it is the hero's arduous movements that link the ordinary street scenes of the massacre with the events at the Louvre. La Môle is pursued relentlessly by Coconnas until he finds refuge with Margot. Significantly, Chéreau describes the saturated imagery of the massacre through the roles of Coconnas and La Môle:

> Coconnas, in a bloody frenzy, showers death all around him. For us, in this film, it shall be the stations of the Cross which La Môle will have to cross, in rags and losing blood, before reaching Margot's room…We shall have to show this pagan yet fanatical period, to show how religious and sensuous it was, show death alongside the pleasures of the flesh.[37]

Finding Margot after their chance encounter in the alleyway, La Môle's return marks Margot's redemption, and their fateful love is sealed. For the first time we hear the musical theme associated with the lovers – a haunting female vocal line accompanied by a choir. With great tenderness, which contrasts starkly with their first brusque encounter, Margot nurses La Môle. She strips off his clothes, using white cloths to soak up huge quantities of blood. At the epicentre of this shot is La Môle's suffering body, naked and beautifully lit as he writhes in pain. Unmistakably, the image of Margot cradling the prostate man in her arms resembles a pietà. Yet, even as La Môle is bound by fate to Margot, he is also powerfully connected to Coconnas. Chéreau's notes, cited above, underline the symbolic importance of these two men in a vivid cinematic account of sin and redemption that draws on pagan and Christian imagery alike.

As in the love tryst in the countryside, Margot's tryst with La Môle is cut short when she is called to Navarre's side. La Môle drags himself back into the streets in a crazed pursuit of Coconnas. In the early light of dawn, surrounded by corpses, the two badly injured men hack at each other with swords until, finally, they collapse together in a heap. When the executioner rescues them from among the dead, the two men are still locked together in an embrace that marks them either as passionate enemies or as lovers.

As previously indicated, from the beginning *La Reine Margot* is structured both by a heterosexual love triangle and by La Môle's and Coconnas' fateful relationship (sealed by their shared bed at the inn). While Margot's relationship with Navarre lacks genuine attachment and her love affair with La Môle is truncated, Coconnas and La Môle forge a friendship from enmity that binds them until death. Returning to the film's recurring theme of the wounded male body, Margot's brief moment of nurturing is matched by a much longer sequence where Coconnas and La Môle are lovingly tended by the burly executioner. This ambiguous and passionate coupling exemplifies the film's underlying affective economy of 'homosocial desire'. An ambivalently sexual relationship that touches on homosexual desires between men, homosocial desire marks a 'glue' between men 'even when its manifestation is hostility or hatred'.[38]

In contrast to the film's weak or truncated heterosexual liaisons, all-male bonds of comradeship and brotherhood (and sworn enmity) are highly charged with sensuality, violence and passion. These bonds are expressed in a tremendous intensity that is focused on the male body. For Sellier, 'the living bodies that touch each other, that are intertwined, whether in pleasure or in a body-to-body struggle, are male bodies'.[39] In a pattern running through many of Chéreau's works, heterosexual unions, female characters and female bodies are sidelined in favour of stronger physical and affective bonds among men; a classic example is the early wrestling scene between Guise and Anjou, which features women along the sidelines. Noting the 'monstrousness' of Médicis and the 'mask-like' or 'mummified' nature of Adjani's performance in *La Reine Margot*, Luc Moullet points out that, for this director, 'the humanity and richness of the male characters seems to contrast with the inhumanity of women'.[40]

This critic specifically mentions Chéreau's early film *L'Homme blessé*, which follows the violent 'coming of age' of a young gay man. Here, teenager Henri (Anglade) develops an obsession with an older man, Jean, who is implicated in a male prostitution ring. As their sexual relationship develops it becomes increasingly violent, ending on Henri's passionate strangulation of the older man during sex. Notably, the two female characters in *L'Homme blessé* are completely sidelined from the narrative: Henri's mother is held at knifepoint by her son seeking money to give to Jean; meanwhile, Jean shows barely any interest in his girlfriend, choosing to have sex with her only in order to provoke Henri.[41]

In *La Reine Margot*, Chéreau's interest in the male body is reflected in bravura performances by male actors and an attention to the faces and bodies of its leading male figures – a process exemplified by the heroic framing of La Môle as the suffering, Christ-like figure. Indeed, the image of the male body in agony recurs at the end of the film with Charles on his deathbed. Anglade's extraordinary performance of the capricious king culminates in this scene of writhing contrition. Charles' face and torso are framed in profile as he arches his body in agony, sweating blood; gradually his white night shirt is completely soaked in blood (just as Margot's gown soaked up La Môle's blood during the massacre).

In a reprise of La Môle's suffering during the massacre, the image of Charles on his deathbed revisits the blood of the victims on the body of the powerful. *La Reine Margot*'s biblical cycle of suffering, vengeance and redemption concludes with the death of Charles – and the predicted early deaths of Anjou and Alençon. During the massacre, the historical roles of perpetrator and victim were personified by Coconnas and La Môle. After Coconnas' contrition and reconciliation with La Môle, the king's body betrays his guilt, linking him into this corporeal bond of punishment and redemption. This bond culminates in the intercutting of the executions of La Môle and Coconnas with Charles (who has the power to pardon them) on his deathbed.

As Charles lies on his deathbed, La Môle and Coconnas (who have been condemned to death for La Môle's association with the book that poisoned the king) are transported in a simple cart to the place of execution. The men's arrival at the scaffold echoes the imagery from the morning after the massacre, with the same blue dawn light and elegaic choral music. Meanwhile, at the Louvre, Margot pleads with the dying Charles for her lover's life, as Coconnas carries the crippled La Môle – who was shot in both knees during their capture – up to the scaffold. Just before his decapitation at the hands of the executioner who had previously healed him, La Môle cries out: 'Margot!' – but it is Coconnas, the repentant killer, who is by his side. After the execution we return to Charles' bedside, as he announces La Môle's death to Margot just before he, too, expires.

In this way, the film's heterosexual and homosocial alliances are conjoined in the film's dénouement. In the film's final scenes the joyous Anjou returns, kissing the handsome Nançay passionately on the mouth as his succession as Henri III is announced. Afterwards, we turn to Margot and Henriette in their private moment of grief with their lovers' decapitated bodies. Following a long-standing macabre fable, Margot departs in a carriage with Orthon, holding the bloody head of La Môle on her lap. Part of a seemingly endless torrent of blood, La Môle's head bleeds into Margot's white gown, staining it. Above, I discussed the centrality of Orthon's angelic gaze during the massacre, and significantly, the page is present in the final scene, declaring to Margot: 'Navarre is waiting for you.' This statement gestures prophetically towards Navarre, who will survive to instate tolerance in a war-torn France.

Within Chéreau's cinematic account of bloody 16th-century France, historical events are dramatised through a condensed cinematic language of colour, lighting, faces and bodies. Rather than an intellectual understanding of the past, we are brought into an intensive proximity to past experience. This immediacy is produced partly through the camera's close attention to the faces and the bodies of the actors. In a complex and confusing narrative, the film addresses the spectator most insistently through its potent corporeal imaging of violence, suffering and death.

The massacre of Saint-Barthélemy as cinematic spectacle relies on the potent expressive nature of violence to instantiate the effects of power visited directly on the body. The literal quality of violence as direct manifestation of despotic power feeds a widespread fascination with spectacles of violence within contexts distant in time or space. Yet *La Reine Margot* mobilises other corporeal metaphors. The film touches upon a common association of the female body with death through Médicis the horrific mother, or the photogenic images of female corpses after the massacre. Another potent image of femininity and death is the death of Navarre's lover Sauve, who dies from poisoned lip balm offered as a powerful aphrodisiac. The young woman's thrashing, terrible death in the throes of passion crystallises a recurring association not only between death and femininity but between sexuality and death.

*La Reine Margot*'s saturated corporeal imagery also foregrounds blood and poison, desire and death. At the time of the film's release, its fascination with blood, desire and death was often equated with potent metaphors about AIDS. The AIDS crisis was at its height during the film's production, and Chéreau's publicly acknowledged homosexuality would suggest a heightened sensitivity to the spreading poison signified by tainted blood. Further, Adjani herself had been 'tainted' by rumours of HIV infection and even death.

Partly taking up influential cultural discourses related to AIDS, *La Reine Margot* consistently juxtaposes desire and violence, the sexual act and death. From the beginning, the wedding festivities are steeped in a rising crescendo of death and desire – Margot, we remember, declares to Guise: 'I want to see the image of my death amidst my pleasure' – culminating in the massacre's explosion of violence. Not limited to late 20th-century discourses of rampant sexuality and danger, these discourses also incorporate earlier cultural sources. In addition to the Romantics, Chéreau draws extensively from the Elizabethan theatre to imagine Renaissance France. The theatrical world of Shakespeare and Marlowe was suffused with sexuality, violence and death. In contrast with the widespread notion of Renaissance as political and cultural 'rebirth', Jonathan Dollimore identifies one element in Renaissance thought that conjoins a broader Western fixation on desire and death. This early modern vision of 'Eros and Thanatos' suggestively sums up key themes in *La Reine Margot*.

> What recurs in early modern writings is the sense of death not simply as the end of desire, nor simply its punishment; shockingly, perversely, death is itself the impossible dynamic of desire. And not just desire; life more generally is animated by the dynamic of death … [E]nergy and movement – ostensibly the essence of life – are more truly the dynamic of its dissolution, the incessant motion, the *driving* force of death.[42]

This chapter has developed a close reading of the film by examining its narrative structure and key elements of its film language – and by drawing out thematic preoccupations such as the film's treatment of death, bodies and sexuality. Many of the points raised in the first two chapters are taken up again in the final chapter's treatment of the film's reception.

### Notes

1    Rosenstone, 'The historical film as real history', pp. 11–12.
2    Cited in Tranchant, Marie-Noëlle and Ferney, Frédéric, 'Patrice Chéreau: "Je fais du cinéma pour filmer des visages"', *Le Figaro*, 13 May 1994.
3    Vincendeau, 'Unsettling memories', p. 32.

4    Grindon, Leger, *Shadows on the Past: Studies in the Historical Fiction Film*, (Philadelphia, 1994), pp. 15–16.

5    For Goubert, with his 'robust good health, the king of France and Navarre stands in sharp contrast to his fragile Valois predecessors, who were indecisive, ostentatious, bedizened with jewels and plumes, and always sickly'. *The Course of French History*, p. 105.

6    This version of the marriage, where the king intervenes, was invented in 1646 by Mézeray, one of the authors of the influential and massive *Histoire de France*. See Viennot, *Marguerite de Valois*, p. 271.

7    Cited in Tranchant and Ferney, 'Patrice Chéreau'.

8    Sedgwick, Eve Kosofsky, *Between Men: English Literature and Male Homosocial Desire* (New York, 1985), p. 2.

9    Significantly, for Barthes Garbo's face (especially in *Queen Christina*) epitomises the myth of an ethereal essence of cinematic beauty. See Barthes, *Mythologies*, pp. 56–57.

10   Comolli, Jean-Louis, 'Historical fiction: a body too much', *Screen* 19/2 (1978), p. 46.

11   Shone, Tom, 'Queen Isabelle', *Sunday Times Magazine*, 20 November 1994, p. 58.

12   Comolli, 'Historical fiction', p. 43.

13   Lefevre, 'Une autre vision', p. 66.

14   Ibid., p. 67.

15   For instance, in Paul Rival's 1929 tract *La folle vie de la Reine Margot* the two women jointly seduce a character called Vitteaux. See Viennot, *Marguerite de Valois*, p. 373.

16   Viennot notes that the outrageous assertions of *Le Divorce satyrique* were revived in several works associated with a post-World War II anti-feminist backlash, and again in the 1980s. See Viennot, *Marguerite de Valois*, pp. 379–393.

17   Sellier, 'La Reine Margot au cinéma', p. 214.

18   Chéreau, 'Director's notes', p. 3.

19   Tranchant and Ferney, 'Patrice Chéreau'.

20   Trilling, Lionel, 'Why we read Jane Austen', in D. Trilling (ed.), *The Last Decade: Essays and Reviews, 1965–75* (Oxford, 1982), pp. 219–220.

21   Brooks, Peter, *History Painting and Narrative: Delacroix's 'Moments'* (Oxford, 1998), p. 30.

22   Riches, David, 'The phenomenon of violence', in D. Riches (ed.), *The Anthropology of Violence* (Oxford, 1986), p. 9.

23   Chéreau, 'Director's notes', p. 2.

24   Riches, 'The phenomenon of violence', p. 7.

25   Ibid., p. 10.

26   Dyer notes that 19th-century Western portraiture and movie lighting derive significantly from North European painting traditions. Borrowing from Rembrandt and Northern European painters, the use of an idealised 'Northern light' in portraiture and in film confers both individuality and 'enlightenment' on the subject. Although both Rembrandt and the Enlightenment follow the events chronicled in *La Reine Margot*, this lighting scheme nonetheless carries these connotations in the present of the film's production. See Dyer, Richard, *White* (London, 1997), pp. 117–119.

27   'Virna Lisi: "J'ai adoré être méchante"', *Le Figaro*, 13 May 1994.

28   Sellier, 'La Reine Margot au cinéma', p. 215.

29   Bronfen, Elisabeth, *Over Her Dead Body: Death, Femininity and the Aesthetic* (Manchester, 1992), p. xi.

30   See Stacey, Jackie and Pearce, Lynne, 'The heart of the matter: feminists revisit romance', in L. Pearce and J. Stacey (eds), *Romance Revisited* (New York, 1995), pp. 17–18.

31   Belsey, Catherine, *Desire: Love Stories in Western Culture* (Oxford, 1994), p. 38.

32   Pearce, Lynne, 'Another time, another place: the chronotope of romantic love in contemporary feminist fiction', in L. Pearce and G. Wisker (eds), *Fatal Attractions* (London, 1998), p. 99.

33   Dyer, *White*, p. 134.

34   Allegations of incest between Marguerite de Valois and her brothers were first circulated publicly in politico-pornographic pamphlets during Valois' own lifetime.

35   Goubert writes of Anjou: 'As a good Valois, he adored pomp, strange festivals, jewels, small animals, and particularly, it is said, young boys – an abominable crime for ordinary mortals in that age. But he did not detest attractive girls either.' See Goubert, *The Course of French History*, p. 99.

36   Sellier, 'La Reine Margot au cinéma', p. 214.

37   Chéreau, 'Director's notes', p. 1.

38   Sedgwick, *Between Men*, p. 2. It is worth noting that Sedgwick focuses on the English novel from the 18th to the mid-19th century. However, in referencing Luce Irigaray's broader discussion of the 'homosocial', Sedgwick implies that this term resonates within other historical periods and cultures.

39   Sellier, 'La Reine Margot au cinéma', p. 216.

40   Mollet, Luc, 'Margot Schindler', *Cahiers du cinéma* 482 (1994), p.41.

41   For an analysis of *L'Homme blessé*, see *Théâtre au cinéma*, p. 30.

42   Dollimore, Jonathan, *Death, Desire and Loss in Western Culture* (London, 1998), p. 76.

# 3   Reception

From the preceding textual reading, in this chapter I turn to the domestic and international reception of *La Reine Margot*. Given the epic scale of Chéreau's production, I pay particular attention to the pre-release publicity that heralded the film's release at Cannes as a national media event. Other elements addressed here include the film's critical reception and box-office and admission figures, both in France and internationally. Broadly speaking, *La Reine Margot* was received most warmly by critics as an auteurist art film; many of the reviews highlight Chéreau's auteurist intervention in the genre. However, even with its huge budget and all-star cast, *La Reine Margot* did not achieve the popular success of its precursor *Cyrano de Bergerac* in France or the United States. Significantly, the film's best admission figures were in Europe, where the film cashed in on its European cast and more favourable markets for art cinema. As a counterpoint to the film's many favourable reviews, a recurring complaint among audiences and critics alike was the film's excessive length and its lack of coherent narrative structure. As a result, Chéreau produced two shorter versions for European and US markets.

### Pre-release publicity

As mentioned in Chapter 1, the promotion of *La Reine Margot* followed strategies for French super-productions developed in the 1980s. In the year prior to its release the film received a major media build-up through coverage of the film's production process and interviews with Chéreau. For instance, in May 1993 (a full year before the film's release) a feature-length article entitled 'Finally, *La Reine Margot!*'[1] appeared in the glossy *Studio Magazine*. Announcing the 'beginning of the filming of Patrice Chéreau with Adjani on May 10', this four-page spread sought to generate public anticipation for the project. Too early to include production stills, the article was illustrated with images of paintings and drawings used by production and costume designers, and a small-scale model of the wedding scene. Accompanying these images were Chéreau's 'Director's notes', poetically conveying his auteurist vision for the film.

Several months later, the July/August issue of the same magazine announced the completion of the first phase of shooting with a six-page full-colour spread. Highlighting the film's prestigious director and all-star cast, the headline read: 'Patrice Chéreau brings together Ajani, Auteuil, Anglade, Perez in LA REINE MARGOT.'[2] The subtitle described the film as 'one of the most ambitious projects [featuring] one of the most exciting line-ups. Here are some of these faces to accompany your dreams.' In keeping with Chéreau's attention to faces, this six-page spread included full-colour 'portraits' of the principal actors in costume. The headlines are reversed into a two-page spread featuring a full-length colour image of Adjani in her sumptuous blue dress from the wedding party on the right-hand page. The star is perched on a stone platform with a pillar behind her, and a few candles can be seen at the top of the left-hand page. In keeping with the film's theatrical look, the image is cloaked in darkness to place dramatic emphasis on the actress. Another small image in the lower left-hand corner depicts Chéreau holding Adjani's head between his hands. Both images work to reinforce Adjani's mythic presence at the centre of the film, as well as Chéreau's guiding role as director.

In the article's next four pages the leading actors are photographed in groups corresponding to the structuring themes of the monstrous family and the love triangle. One two-page spread groups together the Valois as 'a mother and her four children' (Lisi as Médicis surrounded by Anglade, Adjani, Greggory and Rassam). The second spread foregrounds the love triangle with Auteuil as Navarre, Perez as La Môle, and an erotic full-page shot of Adjani holding Auteuil down on the floor. Including only two narrow columns of text, this promotional article furnishes vivid imagery of the actors in role. These two articles from *Studio Magazine* exemplify the film's print media coverage, which frequently included large, ravishing images celebrating the film's distinctive mode of period spectacle.

Pre-release production stills provided a teaser, a lead-up to the shadow play (noted in Chapter 2) between the body of the actor and the myth of the historical persona. Given the centrality of the Adjani/Margot mythology to the project, the film's French film poster featured a full-length image of Adjani in pearls and an off-the-shoulder white dress that is soaked in blood. The actress holds her hands to her face in distress, gazing off-screen at some unknown horror. The background of the poster is in shades of red fading into black, but no 'set' can be seen; this absence of period fittings signals a 'raw' emotional power for the film. Adjani's horrified gaze off the edge of the poster piques the audience's interest in the contemporary gruesome cinematic depiction of Saint-Barthélemy – an infamous historical event familiar to most of the French audience.

Another crucial aspect of the hype surrounding the release of *La Reine Margot* was a wide array of publications addressing the historical figure of Marguerite de Valois. A flurry of commentaries on Valois herself appeared, notably two 1993 publications: a new biography by Janine Garisson[3] alongside Éliane Viennot's *Marguerite de Valois: Histoire d'une femme, histoire d'un mythe*. In 1994 Obres published a new edition of the *Mémoires* of Marguerite de Valois. Several new publications addressed the broader historical context, notably Denis Crouzet's book *La Nuit de la Saint-Barthélemy: Un rêve perdu de la Renaissance*, which also appeared in 1994; moreover, Jean-François Dubost's feature-length article 'La Légende noire de la Reine Margot' was published in the periodical *L'Histoire* in May 1994 to coincide with the film's release. Similarly, newspaper coverage often included brief historical accounts on the period, including Valois 'family trees', chronologies of events, portraits of major historical figures/film characters and reading lists featuring these new publications.

Finally, as prestigious literary adaptations typically generate a revival of the original novel, several new editions of Dumas' novel were published to coincide with the film's release. Flammarion, Gallimard, Pocket and Lgf all published new versions of Dumas' novel. On the cover of the Lgf version (published under the direction of Viennot) is an image of Adjani as Margot. All these new editions include prefaces and other contextual material; the

Pocket edition is especially replete with additional information, including an introduction by Claude Aziza, a chronology of the period covered by the novel, historical documents (including excerpts from Marguerite de Valois' memoirs), a biographical timeline for Dumas and a bibliography. The final element in the edition is a filmography that includes Chéreau's forthcoming film.

If adaptations spark renewed interest in French classic novels and plays, they also prompt a fond return to earlier adaptations. This tendency has been particularly prevalent since the widespread video and DVD availability of earlier films (as well as frequent television broadcast of genre classics such as *Fanfan la tulipe*). Dréville's earlier adaptation of *La Reine Margot* was a frequent point of reference during the pre-release period; for instance, an image of Moreau as Margot appeared on the cover of the 1994 Gallimard edition of Dumas' novel. In the month of the film's release, alongside a feature-length article on Chéreau's forthcoming film, the glossy film magazine *Première* ran an article on Dréville's previous adaptation. Illustrated with an image of the bare-shouldered Moreau as Margot beside her sleeping lover, the article reminds the audience of the scandal surrounding Moreau's nude scene (where the actress famously used a body double) in this 'kitsch adaptation' from 40 years earlier.[4]

Included in this article is background on the original production and an interview with the 88-year-old Dréville, who describes his film as 'light-hearted', in the spirit of Dumas. Dréville comments that Chéreau's version was bound to be very different, 'something more dramatic, more violent or political', but notes that he is 'full of curiosity – and of deference – for the new *Reine*'.[5] In this way, *Première* payed homage to the earlier film while insisting on the specificity of Chéreau's new work. The article also mentioned that, a few days prior to the release of Chéreau's film, the television channel Canal Plus was to broadcast Dréville's 1954 film.[6] It is worth noting that Canal Plus was one of the production companies involved in the 1994 version, and this collaboration in marketing the film reflects a widespread convergence between television and film companies for production and distribution.

The return to older films and cinema lore is part of the industry build-up for the new adaptation. In this way, Chéreau's film is inserted within the popular cultural trajectory of Dumas and the French costume and swashbuckling genres. At the same time, the new *La Reine Margot* is distinguished from the earlier version through Chéreau's auteurist credentials, and the sheer scale of the film as a 1990s super-production: the *Première* article reminds the reader that Dréville's 1954 film required 91 days of filming, and that its relatively high budget for the period amounted to only 1/50th of the cost of Chéreau's film.[7] As part of the promotion machine for the 1994 *La Reine Margot*, the return to Moreau's 'Margot' through images, commentary and gossip also contributed to the shifting mythology of 'la reine Margot'. The circulation of iconic images – an important French actress in historical costume – helped to cement specific versions of the 'Margot' myth in popular memory. The return to Moreau as Margot contributed to a collective anticipation of the elusive Adjani's grand entrance as the next 'Margot'.

## French reception

After this extensive build-up within the French media, *La Reine Margot* was released on 13 May 1994 through the distributor AMLF (known as Pathé since 1999). Such was the success of the film's pre-release publicity campaign that some 80,000 spectators queued up across France for the film's first screening.[8] As part of the film's promotional strategy as high-profile media 'event', its commercial release was timed to coincide with the Cannes Film Festival, where *La Reine Margot* was to represent France. Indeed the film's triumphant opening recalled Truffaut's characterisation of the 'tradition of quality', in which certain ambitious films 'defend the French flag twice a year at Cannes and at Venice [regularly carrying] off medals, golden lions and *grand prix*'.[9] As a high-profile auteurist work, *La Reine Margot* collected the award for Best Actress (Lisi) and the Jury Prize at Cannes. The film also swept the French César awards, winning prizes for Best Actress (Adjani), Best Cinematography (Rousselot), Best Costume Design (Moidele Bickel), Best Supporting Actor (Anglade) and Best Supporting Actress (Lisi).

Much of the French press coverage focused on *La Reine Margot* at the 47th Cannes Festival. In concert with the film's release, the daily and weekly press ran interviews (primarily with Chéreau, but also with Perez, Lisi, Anglade, Greggory, Adjani and Auteuil). Many of the reviews are highly complementary of Chéreau's 'auteurist' vision of Dumas and of Saint-

Barthélemy. For instance, Danièle Heymann of *Le Monde* calls *La Reine Margot* 'a splendid and furious film, where all of Chéreau's powers seem entirely focused. We see his life, his passions, his obsessions. We see his team, which has become a troupe, the three poles of his work – theatre, opera, cinema – reconciled for the first time.'[10] The article foregrounds Chéreau's prestigious theatrical pedigree, emphasising his arrival as a full cinematic 'auteur' with *La Reine Margot* after several previous minor films.

Entitled 'L'opéra funèbre de Chéreau', Heymann's article (like many others) foregrounds the film's dark vision of the French national past; a harsher review describes the film as 'sinister' in comparison with Dumas' light-hearted spirit.[11] Much of the press coverage explicitly links the film's dark and violent vision to the Holocaust and to recent events in the Balkans, Algeria and Rwanda (where the horrific ethnic cleansing had only just occurred at the time of the film's release). The assessment of Chéreau's 'contemporary' vision of Saint-Barthélemy varies between commendations for the film's political relevance[12] and a sceptical response to the film's allegorical imagery. For instance, a review in *Le Figaro* finds Chéreau's parallel between the Holocaust and Saint-Barthélemy unnecessary, ahistorical and anachronistic.[13] A different point comes up in *Globe hebdo*, when Chéreau was asked in an interview if the film's aesthetic treatment of the massacre or its 'fascination with corpses undercuts the film's denunciation of intolerance?' In response, Chéreau retains his 'auteurist' position to insist that ugliness is pointless in painting and in cinema – that, 'in order to look at real monstrosity, it must be beautiful. That doesn't take anything away from the violence or the indignation. Everyone knows that death hypnotizes, like a snake.'[14]

In general, the daily press coverage respectfully acknowledges the scope and ambition of Chéreau's film. Nevertheless, several pointed criticisms emerge in response to *La Reine Margot* as popular cinema. A common complaint concerns the film's confusing narrative which for some lacks a central theme, conflict or character. As a result, for Pierre Billard of *Le Point* the film does not elicit an emotional response.[15] This argument aligns with Chapter 2's discussion of the film's curious lack of emotional centre and its resistance to the affective pleasures of romance and period settings associated with costume film. Interestingly, this point also comes up in Vincent Amiel's review in the specialist film journal *Positif*; whereas most of the specialist film press praises the film, Amiel claims that, although this film is much celebrated for its dynamism, the multiple tensions and constant movement lack a central dramaturgy, a coherence for the spectator.[16] (It is worth noting that Chéreau decided to re-edit his film for its Italian and German releases in August and September, respectively; designed to be more comprehensible, this new version was 140 minutes long, shaving 20 minutes off the original.[17])

A perceptive commentary in *Libération* lauds the spirit of *La Reine Margot*, but notes that Chéreau's 'intellectual project' squares badly with a 'popular film' format.[18] This observation drives home the core contradiction between Chéreau's auteurist vision and the expensive epic's quest for a popular audience. Nonetheless, popular film magazines such as *Première* and *Studio* are for the most part full of praise for Chéreau's film as a glamorous super-production. In addition to the tremendous build-up prior to the film's release, *La Reine Margot* was featured extensively in *Studio Magazine*'s special Cannes edition, which also included an interview with Chéreau, a review and a round-table interview with five of the film's principal actors (Adjani, Anglade, Auteuil, Perez, Greggory). Underlining this work as an 'actor's film', this article describes *La Reine Margot* as 'an encounter of the most exciting actors that French cinema has seen for a long time'.[19] Also, the May 1994 issue of *Le Mensuel du cinéma* featured *La Reine Margot* (including an image of Adjani as Margot) in its Cannes editorial,[20] along with a 24-page dossier (including an interview with Chéreau, a review, an interview with the production designer Jean-Claude Bourlat and a profile of Adjani).

Meanwhile, in the distinctive realm of the specialist film press, the celebration of Chéreau's film by *Cahiers du cinéma* is indicative of a preference for auteurist costume films. The journal featured the film in its editorial and in a 12-page dossier, including an interview with Chéreau and Serge Toubiana's rave review. The case of *Cahiers du cinéma* is key as this influential journal is part of the specialist film press that perpetuates the terms of Truffaut's 1954 indictment of costume film and literary adaptation (see Chapter 1). With the renewed importance of historical fiction and literary adaptation for French cinema in the 1980s and 1990s, specialist film journals such as *Cahiers du cinéma* and *Positif* have retained a crushing disdain for the genre. For instance, the journal ran a lukewarm review of the popular Pagnol adaptations *Jean de Florette* and *Manon des Sources*. Noting Truffaut's earlier indictment of Pagnol and Berri as part of an old-fashioned '*cinéma du Papa*',[21] Toubiana describes Berri as a determined but limited 'artisan' whose films have a certain charm but lack ambition.[22]

This tendency continues in the 1990s, with Annaud's 1992 film *L'Amant* (produced by Berri) being lambasted by critics in the specialist press. Jacques Morice of *Cahiers du cinéma*, for instance, describes Annaud (who has been associated with the rise of the French super-production) as an 'eclectic (opportunistic?) persona'; the film itself is indicted as an 'impersonal' assemblage of cinematic images that is ultimately 'robotic', lacking in feeling and 'very conservative'.[23] Meanwhile, Régis Warnier's *Indochine*, released later in 1992, is written off as 'colonial nostalgia'.[24] Often including personal attacks on the filmmakers, these dismissive reviews stand out in contrast to these films' tremendous popularity among French and international audiences.

In their haughty disdain for costume film, specialist film journals tend to make an exception for recognisably 'auteurist' works such as *La Reine Margot*. The critics of this journal praise Chéreau's film for its auteurist vigour, which 'imposes its own rhythm and energy' on the 'unhappy' and 'heavy' French genre of historical fiction.[25] In the same issue, Thierry Jousse's editorial also explicitly distinguishes *La Reine Margot* from the static 'academic' spectacle of historical fiction: 'Not a gram of academicism here, but on the contrary an energy, a movement that literally pierces the actors.'[26] In terms of the critical support for *La Reine Margot*, producer Berri's own *Germinal* marks a key point of reference.

Both films are super-productions adapting classic French novels and iconic historical periods, and each received significant state subsidy. Berri's epic was released in September 1993, with Chéreau's film following in May, 1994, and both releases were heralded as cinematic and cultural 'events' in France. Each was conceived, financed and marketed through star players associated with iconic literary roles and spectacular, large-scale productions: the ubiquitous Gérard Depardieu as Zola's miner-hero Maheu (alongside singer Renaud as Étienne Lantier) and Adjani in the role of Margot. Yet the differences between the films' critical reception are also telling. While *La Reine Margot* was for the most part welcomed by critics as a fresh auteurist work, *Germinal* was attacked by *Cahiers du cinéma* as state-sanctioned official culture. Praising the popular time-travelling comedy *Les Visiteurs* of 1993 as dynamic and carnivalesque, Jousse lambasted Berri's film as an 'enterprise of vulgarization, the fossilization of literary culture'.[27]

In part, *Germinal* was suspect because of its explicit association with the leftist-nationalist cultural project of the Mitterrand government (see Chapter 1). Nonetheless, due to its iconic source novel and an innovative publicity campaign, the film garnered a respectable FF51,000,000 in France,[28] and brought in over 6,000,000 spectators. Meanwhile, Annaud's *L'Amant* (despised by the specialist press) and *Indochine* each attracted approximately 3,200,000 spectators. *La Reine Margot*, in contrast, received considerable critical acclaim with an emphasis on Chéreau's auteurist achievement. The film's domestic box office was respectable but slightly disappointing with only 2,000,000 spectators.[29] Other period productions released in the early 1990s included *Tous les matins du monde* (2,200,000 admissions), *Le Colonel Chabert* (1,700,000 spectators), *La Fille d'Artagnan* (1,500,000 spectators), *Farinelli* (1995; 1,300,000 spectators).[30] Given its budget of FF140,000,000 *La Reine Margot*'s domestic performance is low compared to these other works – all, with the exception of *Le Colonel Chabert*, much more modest productions.

Despite these differences in critical reception, part of the logic uniting *Cyrano de Bergerac, L'Amant, Indochine, Germinal, La Reine Margot* and *Le Hussard sur le toit* was a French challenge to American cultural hegemony. All these projects received funding through the *avances sur recettes* in order to complete with American blockbusters. Mitterrand's state policy of protection for cultural production was topical in the context of the early 1990s General Agreement on Trade and Tariff (GATT) negotiations with the United States, in which the Americans claimed that this type of state funding amounted to unfair competition. Berri's *Germinal* coincided directly with the GATT negotiations, and inevitably the film was caught up in these debates. On this note, it is significant that in the year of its release *Germinal* was eclipsed in the French market by four Hollywood films: *Aladdin, Jurassic Park, Mrs Doubtfire* and *The Fugitive*.[31] Ironically, by far the most successful French 'historical' film of the early 1990s was the spoof *Les Visiteurs*, in which two medieval thugs are projected forward in time into contemporary France. Lacking the cultural capital to attract state support, this popular slapstick film was the only French production to compete with Hollywood. In 1993 *Les Visiteurs* topped the French market with over 12,600,000 admissions.[32]

International reception

As with the 1950s large-scale productions, a crucial part of the rationale for the French super-productions lay in their appeal with international audiences. Dating back to the surprise international sales of *Jean de Florette* and *Manon des Sources*, these films were conceived as 'quality' exports. Rappeneau's *Cyrano de Bergerac*, for instance, attracted 11,000,000 admissions worldwide,[33] earning some FF50,000,000 abroad (almost as much as its FF60,000,000 domestic box office).[34] Subsequent epics *La Reine Margot* and *Le Hussard sur le toit* were sold to international distributors partly on the basis of this success. In turn, *La Reine Margot* attracted a strong 2,600,000 admissions abroad (more than its domestic audience), achieving its greatest international reception in Europe – notably in Spain and Italy (448,000 admissions in each country), Germany (300,000 admissions) and Belgium (106,000 admissions). The film's performance was also strong in the Canadian French-speaking province of Québec, the film's first non-European release (126,000 admissions), and in Brazil (120,000 admissions).[35]

Given that *La Reine Margot* was a joint production with Italy and Germany and that it featured several well-known Italian actors (Virna Lisi, Claudio Amendola and Asia Argento), its box-office appeal in these countries was expected. The film's excellent reception in Spain, however, was more of a surprise. The casting of singer/actor Miguel Bosè as Guise is one factor, but the film's Spanish distributor, Cine Company, was also credited with this unexpected success.[36] Part of a strategy to fight Hollywood's hegemony not only in France but also across Europe, the French film industry sought to enhance its profile throughout Europe. In 1994 *La Reine Margot* was among the top three French films in Europe (after Kieslowski's *Trois Couleurs Rouge* and *Blanc*). Significantly, *La Reine Margot* topped both *Germinal* and *Les Visiteurs* in the European market, where art film can fare better than French popular cinema.[37]

According to an article in the trade journal *Le Film français*, the European success of *La Reine Margot* arose from the 'sure value' of selling the French national past. The article cites the super-production formula of 'stars, prestigious (and international) supporting roles, costumes, décors, budget, the combination of small stories and grand-scale History'. The importance of the film's international supporting cast can be seen in the Italian poster design, which features a spectacular image from the wedding, with cameo images of the film's stars arranged around the main title; alongside the French stars, these cameos foreground Italian actors Lisi, Amendola and Argento. Also important to the film's European appeal was Chéreau's strong reputation as a theatre director – a profile that is 'more artistic, and therefore more risqué'.[38] All these factors contributed to the film's considerable European pre-sales, which are almost obligatory for this type of project: indeed, La Reine Margot covered almost 25% of its costs through international agreements before opening in France.[39]

In the United Kingdom, La Reine Margot (released in January 1995) was the top foreign-language film of 1995 with 146,000 admissions,[40] earning over £600,000.[41] The film was also nominated as 'Best Film not in the English Language' at the 1996 BAFTA awards. The critical response to La Reine Margot in the British press was generally favourable, with an overall focus on the film's Gallic excesses of sexuality and violence. As a French export, La Reine Margot was promoted in the United Kingdom partly as a risqué spectacle of an oversexed Renaissance queen. Headlines included 'Adjani woos Cannes with sex and death' (The Times), 'Bodices and bloodstains' (The Daily Telegraph), 'Margot: a royal in search of a roll' (Independent on Sunday), 'Queens have all the fun' (Sunday Telegraph) and 'Queen of Tarts' (The Mail on Sunday). In the British glossy film magazine Première, the film's auteurist and popular dimensions are encapsulated in the headline 'A splendid royal bodice-ripper with brains'.[42] The royal angle is also frequently cited in a country still titillated by the exploits of its own royal family (including Princess Diana) in 1995.

La Reine Margot also garnered critical acclaim in the specialist film journal Sight and Sound and in the trade journal Screen International. Respected film critic Jonathan Romney's thoughtful review compares Chéreau's work with Schindler's List; ultimately, Romney prefers La Reine Margot, where historical distance allows for a different experience of historical spectacle: 'There's a sense of horror, certainly – no film has quite evoked such a sense of the randomness and sheer entropy of mass bloodshed. But we also feel a peculiar relish, an ecstatic immersion in the lush materiality of it all.' Yet like the critics of Cahiers du cinéma, Romney goes on to distinguish Chéreau's film from previous costume film: 'It's a costume drama for anyone who hated A Man for all Seasons or any of those films where you'd get 20 minutes of carousing fustian before being admitted to the private quarters of Cardinal Wolsey.'[43] In the United Kingdom, as in France, Chéreau's auteurist achievement functions alongside a more popular celebration of the film's full measure of blood and guts, sex and death.

Chéreau's film was released with an 'R' rating in the United States in December 1994 with the English title *Queen Margot*. Given the international dominance of Hollywood, US critical reception and box-office figures are commonly considered as a crucial indicator of a film's industrial performance. A nomination for the minor award of Best Costume Design at the 1995 Academy awards helped to garner some publicity, but the film received a generally lukewarm reception in the United States. This trend began with the first American review, published in *Variety* after the film's triumphant Cannes première. Long before the film's US release, Todd McCarthy lambasted Chéreau's film as a self-indulgent, incoherent and overly violent film.

> Sprawling, bloody costumer about the dastardly deeds of 16th-century French royalty is a frenzy of religious conflict, personal betrayal, raw passion and enough killing for all three parts of 'The Godfather'. Unlike the gangster epic, however, this adaptation...doesn't generate any fascination for its murderous characters, and is a mostly unpleasant chore to slog through. With its star-laden cast and heavy promotion, Claude Berri's latest jumbo-budget period piece may fly commercially in Europe, but U.S. [box-office] will undoubtedly be closer to 'Germinal' than to 'Jean de Florette'.[44]

In response to this type of critique, Chéreau was obliged to re-edit the film, trimming down its complex plot and reducing the graphic violence. From an original version of 160 minutes' duration (which had been cut down by 20 minutes for the German and Italian releases), Chéreau produced a new version of 135 minutes for the US release. On the basis of American test audience feedback that the film was too long and confusing, Miramax (the US distributor) asked Chéreau to re-edit the film. As a result, the director made 190 cuts and 24 additions (including new elements of the soundtrack by Bregovic). For those not familiar with the historical period, extensive intertitles were added at the beginning, and a new ending was filmed to foreground Adjani. The most dramatic cuts were to the extensive massacre scenes and the gruesome death of Charles IX, which were both cut back by half.[45] The major goal of this new edit for the US market was to foreground Adjani/Margot and her love affair with La Môle.

Within the French press, this incidence of US 'censorship' produced a flurry of sardonic headlines and commentaries. For instance, a brief article in *Le Figaro* noted that 'Patrice Chéreau's film has undergone a slight facelift to conform to American criteria of beauty'.[46] Ultimately, however, most press commentaries concluded that this new version was slightly more coherent than the original, while retaining the integrity of Chéreau's vision. An article in *Le Monde*, for instance, argued that the new version retained the film's auteurist aura; it reported that Chéreau continually altered his theatre productions even after the première – and that, after all, François Truffaut had continued to rework *Les deux anglaises et le continent*, even after its release.[47]

The American version of the film was launched in New York as *Queen Margot*, earning commendations from the influential New York press.[48] In the *New York Times*, for instance, Janet Maslin critiqued the film's confusing storyline, but commended the film's 'painterly style' and the performances of Lisi, Adjani, Anglade and Auteuil.[49] Yet, even with the distributor Miramax (a company that had earned a reputation for unprecedented success in promoting international art cinema in the United States[50]), *Queen Margot* brought in a only disappointing 300,000 spectators in American markets.[51]

Although *La Reine Margot* did not perform particularly well in the United States, the hint of scandal inevitably boosted the film's profile in France. While the French press sneered at American 'censorship', the distributor AMLF harnessed this publicity to remarket the film in the domestic market in an attempt to enhance its initial poor performance. Indeed, a new poster was produced for the second release, featuring Adjani in her sumptuous blue dress. At this time, the press also reported that the shorter version of the film had facilitated a reconciliation between Chéreau and producer Berri (who had been angry at the length of the Cannes version); in France (as reported by *Le Figaro*) the producer does not have the right to ask for changes to the films that s/he finances.[52] The new version was pleasing to Berri (and to other financiers) – in part for the pragmatic reason that the shorter version of 135 minutes' duration allowed for four (rather than three) screenings daily.

Although Chéreau's film did not perform as well in the United States as the producers had hoped, its reception in Europe (and indeed in the United Kingdom, Quebec and Brazil) underlines the significance of diverse international markets for costume film. The slight absurdity of the re-

release of an American version of *La Reine Margot* in France underlines the international dimensions of this emphatically 'French' mythic media event.

## Notes

1   'Tournage: *La Reine Margot* enfin!', *Studio Magazine* 73 (1993), pp. 60–63.
2   'Patrice Chéreau réunit Adjani, Auteuil, Anglade, Perez dans LA REINE MARGOT', *Studio Magazine* 76 (1993), pp. 90–95.
3   Garisson, Janine, *Marguerite de Valois* (Paris, 1994).
4   For a commentary on Moreau's portrayal of Margot, see Vincendeau, *Stars and Stardom*, p. 122.
5   Bernard, Jean-Jacques, 'Moreau', *Première* 206 (1994), p. 81.
6   Ibid., p. 83.
7   Ibid., p. 82.
8   Rouchy, Marie-Elisabeth, 'Sacre à la tronçonneuse', *Télérama* 28 December 1994, p. 20.
9   Truffaut, 'A certain tendency', p. 255.
10  Heymann, Danièle, 'L'opéra funèbre de Chéreau: Cannes sous le choc de la Reine Margot', *Le Monde*, 15/16 May 1994, pp. 1, 8.
11  Multeau, Norbert, 'Margot jetée aux lions', *Valeurs actuelles*, 17 May 1994, p. 57.
12  See, for instance, Buob, Jacques, 'Plus dur que l'opéra', *L'Express*, 12 May 1994, p. 116.
13  Baignères, Claude, 'Gadget Renaissance', *Le Figaro*, 14/15 May 1994.
14  Jonquet, '*La Reine Margot* vaut-elle cette messe?', p. 34.
15  Billard, Pierre, 'Festival de Cannes', *Le Point*, 17 May 1994, p. 103.
16  Amiel, Vincent, '*La Reine Margot*', *Positif* 401/402 (July/August 1994), pp. 30–31.
17  Rouchy, 'Sacre à la tronçonneuse', p. 20.
18  Lefort, Gérard and Seguret, Olivier, 'Au plus près de Margot', *Libération*, 14 May 1994, p. 23.
19  Lavoignat, Jean-Pierre and D'Yvoire, Christophe, 'Le choeur de la Reine Margot', *Studio Magazine* 87 (1994), p. 70.
20  Roth-Bettoni, Didier, 'Cannes, déjà', *Le Mensuel du cinéma* 17 (1994), p. 1.
21  See Williams, *Republic of Images*, pp. 281–282.
22  Toubiana, Serge, 'L'Opéra Pagnol', *Cahiers du cinéma* 387 (1986), pp. 49–51.
23  Morice, Jacques, 'L'Amant', *Cahiers du cinéma* 453 (1992), p. 72.
24  Jousse, Thierry, 'Indochine', *Cahiers du cinéma* 455/456 (1992), p. 35.
25  Toubiana, 'Complot de famille', p. 10.
26  Jousse, Thierry, 'La Reine et le fou', *Cahiers du cinéma* 479/80 (1994), p. 5.
27  Jousse, Thierry, 'Vous avez dit populaire?', *Cahiers du cinéma* 473 (1993), p. 5. For an analysis of the debates surrounding *Germinal*, see Cousins, Russell, 'The heritage film and cultural politics: *Germinal* (Berri, 1993)', in P. Powrie (ed.), *French Cinema in the 1990s: Continuity and Difference* (Oxford, 1999), pp. 25–36.
28  Heymann, Danièle and Murat, Pierre, *L'année du cinéma 1994* (Paris, 1994), p. 250.
29  '*La Reine Margot* repart au triomphe dans sa nouvelle version', *Le Film français*, 2 December 1994, p. 6.

30  Statistics taken from Powrie (ed), *French Cinema in the 1990s*, pp. 258–263.
31  Heymann and Murat, *L'année du cinéma 1994*, p. 250.
32  Ibid., p. 239.
33  *Unifrance Film International Newsletter* 2 (1995), p. 13.
34  Condon, 'Cinema', p. 214.
35  All foreign admissions figures are taken from Sonsino, Thomas, '*Queen Margot:* a worldwide hit', *Unifrance Film International Newsletter* 2 (1995), p. 16.
36  See 'Les outils de la reconquête', *Le Film français*, 3 November 1995, p. 23.
37  'Top 10 des films en français en Europe pour 1994', *Le film français*, 3 November 1995, p. 23.
38  '"*La Reine Margot*": la valeur sûre du film de patrimoine', *Le Film français*, 3 November 1995, p. 24
39  Ibid., p. 24.
40  "*La Reine Margot*": la valeur sûre du film de patrimoine', p. 16.
41  *Centre national de la cinématographie* 260 (1996), p. 27.
42  Errigo, Angie, '*La Reine Margot*', *Première* (January 1995), p. 12.
43  Romney, Jonathan, 'The joy of excess', *New Statesman and Society*, 13 January 1995, p. 3.
44  McCarthy, 'Queen Margot', *Variety*, 23–29 May 1994, p. 53.
45  'L'Amérique sauve *Margot!*', *Le Figaro*, 14 November 1994.
46  '*La Reine Margot* revue et corrigée', *Le Figaro*, 17–18 December 1994.
47  Frodon, Jean-Michel, 'Margot II, égale à elle-même', *Le Monde*, 19 December 1994.
48  See Schmitt, Olivier, 'Margot à la conquête de New-York', *Le Monde*, 12 December 1994.
49  Maslin, Janet, '*Queen Margot*', *New York Times*, 9 December 1994, p. D9.
50  On Miramax as a 'major independent', see Wyatt, Justin, 'Economic constraints/economic opportunities: Robert Altman as auteur', in *The Velvet Light Trap* 30 (Fall 1996), pp. 59–65.
51  Sonsino, '*Queen Margot*: a worldwide hit', p. 16.
52  '*La Reine Margot* revue et corrigée'.

# Conclusion

*La Reine Margot* was subsequently released in France on video (1995) and on DVD (Pathé, 1999); in France, the 'version inédite' runs for two hours and 23 minutes. Bregovic's original soundtrack for *La Reine Margot* was also released on audio CD by PolyGram Music/Renn Productions in 1994. Following the ongoing fascination with new versions of previously adapted literary classics, a television adaptation of *La Reine Margot* was produced in 2001. This production was directed by Steven Shank, and was filmed at the Abbaye de Villers-la-Ville in Belgium.

With *La Reine Margot*, the cycle of historical 'super-productions' of the late 1980s and early 1990s had almost run its course. The last was Jean-Paul Rappeneau's three-hour epic *Le Hussard sur le toit* from 1995. Starring Juliette Binoche and Olivier Martinez, this lush production from the director of *Cyrano de Bergerac* adapted Jean Giono's classic novel. This romantic 19th-century narrative featured the stunning scenery of Provence. With a budget of FF176,000,000,[1] *Le Hussard sur le toit* was hailed as the most expensive French film of all time – a claim made previously of *Jean de Florette*, *Cyrano de Bergerac* and *Germinal*. Like the preceding super-productions, *Le Hussard sur le toit* was charged with challenging Hollywood hegemony in France.[2] However, it had a mixed critical reception and achieved some 2.4 million admissions.[3] This particular style of historical super-production was closely associated with the Mitterrand presidency, which lost popularity in the early 1990s; Jacques Chirac was elected as president in 1995. The lukewarm box office of *La Reine Margot* and *Le Hussard sur le toit* perhaps signalled an exhaustion or disenchantment with formula of epic cinema as national 'media event'.

Intriguingly, he film following most directly in the footsteps of *La Reine Margot* was the 1997 British biopic *Elizabeth*.[4] From Indian director Shekhar Kapur, the film highlights the young queen's sexuality against the sectarian violence of 16th-century England. *Elizabeth*'s crepuscular lighting scheme, creeping camerawork and graphic sex and violence correspond closely with Chéreau's cinematic aesthetic and his dark vision of the French Renaissance. A subsequent ultra-violent French epic, Luc Besson's 1999 *Jeanne d'Arc/Messenger: The Story of Joan of Arc,* ambitiously takes up the torch of mythic female figures from the French past.

However, *Jeanne d'Arc* explodes the idea of a specifically 'French' heritage production. The film's diverse international cast includes non-French supermodel Milla Jovovich as the iconic French heroine, American stars Dustin Hoffman, Faye Dunaway and John Malkovich, and French actors Vincent Cassel and Pascal Greggory. A distant cousin to the aestheticised violence of *La Reine Margot, Jeanne d'Arc* belongs more to a new generation of transnational mythic epic such as *Gladiator* (2000) or *Troy* (2004) featuring computer-generated imagery. Like the 1950s sprawling epics such as *Ben-Hur* (1959), these works projects feature hybrid international casts, spectacular sets and casts of thousands, and are conceived as transnational 'event' films.

Meanwhile, in France smaller-scale costume films continued to be produced from the mid-1990s. By tracing some of the subsequent appearances of the major actors of *La Reine Margot* it is possible to identify several different modes of production. Vincent Perez, who has been closely associated with period film through his roles in *Cyrano de Bergerac, Indochine* and *La Reine Margot,* appeared with Daniel Auteuil in the swashbuckling romps *Le Bossu* in 1997 and the 2003 remake of *Fanfan la tulipe.* These works continue in the playful popular entertainment tradition of the original *Fanfan la tulipe* and *Cyrano de Bergerac.* In contrast with Chéreau's sombre *La Reine Margot,* they return to a more light-hearted Romantic tradition; other major swashbuckling productions included the television productions *Le Compte de Monte Cristo* (1998) and *Les Misérables* (2000), and the 1998 American version of *The Man in the Iron Mask.*

Alongside with the resilient, masculine of films *de cape et d'épée* genre, many subsequent 1990s productions foregrounded female desire and experience through adaptations of classic French novels or historical biographies. Following on from *Madame Bovary, L'Amant* and *Indochine* from the early 1990s, subsequent works of this type included Claude Berri's *Lucie Aubrac* (1997), *Les Enfants du siècle* (1999) and *La Veuve de Saint-Pierre* (2000). As with Adjani's mythic presence in *La Reine Margot,* these films are conceived around the iconic presence of French actresses such as Catherine Deneuve (*Indochine*), Isabelle Huppert (*Madame Bovary*) and – especially – Juliette Binoche (*Le Hussard sur le toit, La Veuve de Saint-Pierre* (2000), *Les Enfants du siècle*). Finally, Adjani appeared in the 2001 adaptation *La Repentie*. Directed by Læticia Masson, *La Repentie* (along with Diane Kurys' account of the writer Georges Sand, *Les Enfants du siècle*) is significant as a film directed by a woman.

Since *La Reine Margot*, Adjani has continued her policy of relative seclusion, appearing in only four leading roles: the American 1996 remake of the French classic *Diabolique* (1996), *La Repentie, Adolphe* (2002) and Jean-Paul Rappeneau's *Bon Voyage* (2002). Based on the critical success of *La Reine Margot*, Chéreau has produced several critically acclaimed films, including *Ceux qui m'aiment prendront le train, Intimacy* and *Son frère*. Returning to the spare, harsh theatrical style of *L'Homme blessé*, these subsequent films continue in an exploration of the male body and male psyche through passionate relationships between men. Chéreau has not opted to return to historical fiction, and *La Reine Margot* marks the pinnacle of his filmmaking career to date. For Adjani, the role of Margot encapsulated the mythic heights of an extraordinary and uneven stardom.

### Notes

1   'La plus chère des superproductions "à la française"', *Les Echos*, 20 September 1995.
2   Ibid.
3   Powrie, *French Cinema in the 1990s*, p. 261.
4   Film critic Philip French explicitly links *Elizabeth* with *La Reine Margot*. See French, Philip, 'Another fine Bess', *The Observer Review*, 4 October 1998, p. 6.

# Appendix 1: Credits

*La Reine Margot*
France/Germany/Italy 1994
Director: Patrice Chéreau

Certificate 18
Distributor: AMLF
Production Companies: Renn Productions/France 2 Cinéma/D.A. Films (France);
   NEF Filmproduktion/Gmb H/Degeto (Germany); R.C.S. Films and TV (Italy)
With the participation of Centre National de la Cinématographie and Canal Plus
Supported by the European Council's Eurimages Fund
Executive producer: Pierre Grunstein
Production coordinator: Pierre Trémouille
Production manager: Jean-Claude Bourlat
Unit production managers: Catherine Pierrat; Alain Artur
Location production manager: Jean-René Coulon
Second unit director: Jérôme Enrico
Assistant directors: Jérôme Enrico; Emmanuel Hamon; Dominique Furge;
   Portugal: João Pedro Ruivo; Casting: France: Margot Capelier; Extras: Pascal
   Géraud; Germany: Ann Dorthe Braker; Italy: Mirta Guarnaschelli;
   Screenplay/adaptation: Danièle Thompson, Patrice Chéreau; Based on the novel
   by Alexandre Dumas; Dialogue: Danièle Thompson; Script supervisor: Suzanne
   Durrenberger; Director of photography: Philippe Rousselot; Camera operators:
   Marc Koninckx, Jean-Pierre Baronsky; Optical effects: Frédéric Moreau; Editors:
   François Gédigier, Hélène Viard; Production designers: Richard Peduzzi, Olivier
   Radot; Set decorator: Sophie Martel; Special effects: Georges Demetrau;
   Costume design: Moidele Bickel; Costume supervisor: Jean-Daniel Vuillermoz;
   Make-up design: Kuno Schlegelmilch, Thi-Loan Nguyen; Special make-up
   effects: Viktor Leitenbaueur; Hair design: Kuno Schlegelmilch, Fabienne
   Bressan; Wigs: Fabienne Bressan; Special effects: Viktor Leitenbaueur; Music:
   Goran Bregovic; Song: 'Elohi' by Ofra Haza; Goran Bregovic; performed by
   Ofra Haza; Sound design: Guillaume Sciama, Dominique Hennequin; Dialogue
   editor: Sylvie Gadmer; ADR editor: Michel Filippi; Foley editor: Pascal Chauvin;
   Sound mixer: Joël Rangon; Sound effects editors: Gérard Hardy, Christian Dior;
   Advisers: Arms: Christophe Maratier; Animals: Pierre Cadéac; Stunt
   coordinator: Philippe Guégan; Fencing master: Raoul Billerey; Horsemanship
   supervisor: Mario Luraschi; Animal manager: François Hardy

With the technical participation of the Théâtre des Amandiers - Nanterre

Cast: Isabelle Adjani: Marguerite de Valois; Daniel Auteuil: Henri de Navarre; Jean-Hugues Anglade: Charles IX; Vincent Perez: La Môle; Virna Lisi: Catherine de Médicis; Dominique Blanc: Henriette de Nevers; Pascal Greggory: Anjou; Claudio Amendola: Coconnas; Miguel Bosè: Guise; Asia Argento: Charlotte de Sauve; Julien Rassam: Alençon; Thomas Kretschmann: Nançay; Jean-Claude Brialy: Coligny; Jean-Philippe Ecoffey: Condé; Albano Guaetta: Orthon; Johan Leysen: Maurevel; Dörte Lyssewski: Marie Touchet; Michelle Marquais: Nurse; Laura Marsac: Antoinette; Alex Nitzer/Barbet Schroeder: Advisers; Emmanuel Salinger: Du Bartas; Jean-Marac Stehle: Innkeeper; Otto Taussig: Mendès; Bruno Todeschini: Armagnac; Tolsty: Hangman; Bernard Verley: Cardinal; Ulrich Wildgruber: René; Extras: Laurent Arnal, Gerard Berlioz, Christophe Bernard, Marian Blicharz, Daniel Breton, Pierre Brilloit, Valeria Bruni-Tedeschi, Cécile Caillaud, Marc Citti, Grégoire Colin, Erwan Dujardin, Jean Douchet, Philippe Duclos, Marina Golovine, Zygmunt Kargol, Carlos Lopez, Orazio Massaro, Roman Massine, Charles Nelson, Bernard Nissile, Julie-Anne Rauth, Jean-Michel Tavernier, Béatrice Toussaint, Mélanie Vaudaine, Nicolas Vaude

14,512 feet
162 minutes

Dolby stereo
In colour

# Appendix 2: Historical timeline

| | |
|---|---|
| 1545 | Council of Trent (commonly seen as the onset of the Counter-Reformation) |
| 1553 | birth of Marguerite de Valois |
| 1559 | death of Henri II of France, coronation of François II (married to Mary Stuart, Queen of Scots) |
| | Élisabeth de Valois, eldest daughter of Henri II and Catherine de Médicis, married to Philip II of Spain |
| 1560 | death of François II, coronation of Charles IX (under the Regency of his mother, Catherine de Médicis) |
| 1562–1563 | first War of Religion |
| 1566 | beginning of Dutch rebellion against the Spanish occupation of Flanders |
| 1566–1568 | second War of Religion |
| 1568–1569 | third War of Religion |
| 1570 | Peace of Saint-Germain |
| 1572 | marriage between Marguerite de Valois and Henri de Navarre (18 August) |
| | assassination of Coligny (22 August) |
| | massacre of Saint-Barthélemy (24–28 August) |
| 1573 | fourth War of Religion |
| | Henri d'Anjou becomes king of Poland |
| 1574 | Malcontent faction conspires to place Alençon on the throne instead of Anjou |
| | trial of Navarre, Alençon, La Môle and Coconnas |
| | Marguerite publishes le Mémoire justificatif in defence of Navarre |
| | execution of Coconnas and La Môle (30 April) |
| | death of Charles IX from tuberculosis (end of May) |
| | Henri d'Anjou returns from Poland to become Henri III of France |
| 1575 | fifth War of Religion |
| | flight of Alençon from the French court |
| | Marguerite de Valois under house arrest at the Louvre (until 1577) |
| 1576 | Henri de Navarre flees the French court for his own territories and renounces Catholicism |
| 1577 | sixth War of Religion |
| | Marguerite travels to Flanders to liaise with Dutch Protestant rebels on behalf of the Malcontents' plan to place Alençon on the throne |
| 1578 | Marguerite joins Henri de Navarre in Gascogne |
| 1580 | seventh War of Religion |

| | |
|---|---|
| 1584 | death of Alençon (ending the Malcontent plots against Henri III) |
| 1585 | eighth War of Religion |
| | Marguerite intervenes in the religious wars from Agen, and is forced to flee to Carlat |
| 1586 | alienated from Henri III, Catherine de Médicis and Henri de Navarre, Marguerite is sequestered from public life at Usson (where she remains until 1605) |
| 1588 | defeat of the Spanish Armada amidst hostilities with England |
| 1589 | death of Catherine de Médicis |
| 1590 | assassination of Henri III and recognition of Henri de Navarre as legitimate heir to the French throne |
| | Navarre pressured to convert to Catholicism |
| 1593 | Navarre converts to Catholicism and Henri IV is crowned king of France at Chartres |
| 1594 | Henri IV arrives in Paris and begins the pacification of the realm |
| | Marguerite begins writing her *Mémoires* |
| 1598 | Edict of Nantes, granting French Protestants freedom of conscience, equal rights and freedom to worship in many specified places |
| 1599 | annulment of the marriage between Marguerite and Henri IV |
| | Marguerite officially recognised as '*la [reine Marguerite]*' |
| 1600 | marriage between Henri IV and Marie de Médicis |
| 1601 | birth of dauphin Louis |
| 1605 | Marguerite's return to Paris |
| 1607 | Marguerite takes up residence in her famous palace on the rue de la Seine |
| 1610 | assassination of Henri IV |
| | Marie de Médicis becomes regent for her young son Louis XIII |
| 1614 | age of majority of Louis XIII |
| | Marguerite writes the *Discours docte et subtil* |
| 1615 | death of '*la reine Marguerite*' |

# Appendix 3: Adjani filmography

*Le Petit bougnat* (Bernard Toublanc-Michel, 1969)

*L'École des femmes* (Raymond Rouleau, 1973)

*La Gifle* (Claude Pinoteau, 1974)

*Ondine* (Raymond Rouleau, 1975)

*L'Histoire d'Adèle H.* (François Truffaut, 1975)

*Le Locataire* (Roman Polanski, 1976)

*Barocco* (André Téchiné, 1976)

*Violette et François* (Jacques Rouffio, 1976)

*Driver* (Walter Hill, 1977)

*Nosferatu, Fantôme de la nuit* (Werner Herzog, 1978)

*Les Soeurs Brontë* (André Téchiné, 1978)

*Possession* (Andrzej Zulawski, 1980)

*Clara et les chics types* (Jacques Monnet, 1980)

*Quartet* (James Ivory, 1980)

*L'Année prochaine si tout va bien* (Jean-Loup Hubert, 1981)

*Tout feu tout flamme* (Jean-Paul Rappeneau, 1981)

*Antonieta* (Carlos Saura, 1982)

*Mortelle randonnée* (Claude Miller, 1982)

*L'Été meurtrier* (Jean Becker, 1982)

*Subway* (Luc Besson, 1984)

*Ishtar* (Elaine May, 1985)

*Camille Claudel* (Bruno Nuytten, 1987)

*Toxic Affair* (Philomene Esposito, 1992)

*La Reine Margot* (Patrice Chéreau, 1994)

*Diabolique* (Jeremiah Chechik, 1996)

*La Repentie* (Lætitia Masson, 2001)

*Adolphe* (Benoît Jacquot, 2002)

*Bon Voyage* (Jean-Paul Rappeneau, 2002)

*Monsieur Ibrahim et les fleurs du Coran* (2003)

# Appendix 4: Chéreau filmography

*La Chaire de l'orchidée* (1974)

*Judith Therpauve* (1978)

*L'Homme blessé* (1983)

*Hôtel de France* (1986)

*Le Temps et la chambre* (1992)

*La Reine Margot* (1994)

*Ceux qui m'aiment prendront le train* (1998)

*Intimacy/Intimité* (2001)

*Son frère* (2003)

*Gabrielle* (2005)

# Appendix 5: Selected bibliography

Andrew, Geoff, 'Isabelle époque', *Time Out*, 11–18 January 1995, pp. 23–26.

Austin, Guy, *Contemporary French Cinema: An Introduction* (Manchester: Manchester University Press, 1996).

de la Bretèque, François, 'Le film en costumes: un bon objet?', *Cinémaction* 65 (1992), pp. 111–122.

Barthes, Roland, *Mythologies* (London: Paladin, 1973).

Bronfen, Elisabeth, *Over Her Dead Body: Death, Femininity and the Aesthetic* (Manchester: Manchester University Press, 1992).

Brooks, Peter, *History Painting and Narrative: Delacroix's 'Moments'*, Legenda European Humanities Research Centre Special Lecture Series 2 (Oxford: Information Press, 1998).

Chéreau, Patrice, 'Director's Notes', *La Reine Margot*, English press book, 1994.

Comolli, Jean-Louis, 'Historical fiction: a body too much', *Screen* 19/2 (1978), pp. 41–53.

Crouzet, Denis, *La Nuit de la Saint-Barthélemy: Un rêve perdu de la Renaissance* (Paris: Fayard, 1994).

Dollimore, Jonathan, *Death, Desire and Loss in Western Culture* (London: Penguin, 1998).

Dubost, Jean-François, 'La Légende noire de la Reine Margot', *L'Histoire* 177 (1994), pp. 8–16.

Dumas, Alexandre, *La Reine Margot* (Paris: Pocket, 1994).

Dyer, Richard, *White* (London: Routledge, 1997)

Goubert, Pierre, *The Course of French History* (London: Routledge, 1984).

Grindon, Leger, *Shadows on the Past: Studies in the Historical Fiction Film* (Philadelphia: Temple University Press, 1994).

Guibbert, Pierre, 'Le film de cape et d'épée', *CinémAction* 68 (1993), pp. 154–159.

Hayward, Susan, *French National Cinema* (London: Routledge, 1993).

Heymann, Danièle and Murat, Pierre, *L'année du cinéma 1994* (Paris: Calmanne-Lévy, 1994).

Holt, Mack P., *The French Wars of Religion, 1562–1629* (Cambridge: Cambridge University Press, 1995).

Lalanne, Jean-Marc, 'Isabelle Adjani, en quelques états', *Le Mensuel du cinéma* 27 (1994), pp. 68–71.

Nora, Pierre (ed.), *Realms of Memory: The Construction of the French Past* (New York: Columbia University Press, 1996).

Porter, Roy and Teich, Mikulás (eds), *Romanticism in National Context* (Cambridge: Cambridge University Press, 1988).

Powrie, Phil (ed.), *French Cinema in the 1990s: Continuity and Difference* (Oxford: Oxford University Press, 1999).

Prédal, René, *Le Cinéma français depuis 1945* (Paris: Éditions Nathan, 1991).

Reader, Keith (1993) 'Le phénomène Cyrano: perceptions of French cinema in Britain', *Franco-British Studies* 15, pp. 3–8.

*La Reine Margot*, British Press Book, 1995.

Riches, David (ed.), *The Anthropology of Violence* (Oxford: Basil Blackwell, 1986).

Rosenstone, Robert A., 'The historical film as real history', *Film-Historia* 5/1 (1999), pp. 5–23.

Sedgwick, Eve Kosofsky, *Between Men: English Literature and Male Homosocial Desire* (New York: Columbia University Press, 1985).

Sellier, Geneviève, 'La Reine Margot au cinéma: Jean Dréville (1954) et Patrice Chéreau (1994)', in O. Krakovitch, G. Sellier and E. Viennot (eds), *Femmes de pouvoir: Mythes et fantasmes* (Paris: l'Harmattan, 2001), pp. 205–218.

Sutherland, N.M., *The Massacre of Saint Bartholomew and the European Conflict 1559–1572* (London: Macmillan, 1973).

*Théâtre au cinéma: Patrice Chéreau, Jean Genet, Bernard-Marie Koltès*, festival publication vol. 10/10th festival 17–30 March, Bobigny (Bobigny: Le Magic Cinéma, la Ville de Bobigny and the Conseil de la Seine-Saint Denis, 1999).

Toubiana, Serge, 'La Reine Margot: complot de famille', *Cahiers du cinéma* 479/80 (1994), pp. 9–11.

Truffaut, François, 'A certain tendency of the French cinema', in B. Nichols (ed.), *Movies and Methods* (Berkeley: University of California Press, 1976), pp. 224–237.

*Unifrance Film International Newsletter* 2 (1995).

de Valois, Marguerite, *Mémoires et autres écrits de Marguerite de Valois la reine Margot*, edited and with an introduction by Yves Cazaux (Mayenne: Mercure de France, 1971).

Viennot, Éliane, *Marguerite de Valois: Histoire d'une femme, histoire d'un mythe* (Paris: Éditions Payot & Rivages, 1993).

Vincendeau, Ginette, 'Unsettling memories', *Sight and Sound* (July 1995), pp. 30–32.

Vincendeau, Ginette, *Stars and Stardom in French Cinema* (London: Continuum, 2000).